THE *8-STEP* GUIDE
To Boosting Your Creativity
Through A Personal Retreat

DAVID A. BOSSERT

Interior design and layout by Nancy Levey-Bossert
Cover Design: Beach Design
Cover photos: David A. Bossert

Edited and Copy Edited by Lia Ottaviano

Set in Minion 3, Century Gothic Pro used courtesy of Adobe Typekit, SignPainter, Trademark by Jroh Creative, New Press Eroded by Galdino Otten

Printed in Korea

First Edition: September 2024

ISBN: 979-8987058930

Library of Congress Control Number: 2024931240

Visit www.theoldmillpress.com

Dedicated
to my family:

— ✑ —

Nancy, Sydney, and Marlee

— ✑ —

Whose love and support
encouraged my personal retreats over the decades.

— Table of Contents —

—Introduction—

During a challenging phase in my life, I faced a series of personal tragedies that lasted several years. My brother and then my father passed away. I lost a third of my family in less than eighteen months. It was an incredibly difficult time, but my annual personal retreat played a pivotal role in ensuring a positive outcome. Without the discipline and skillset I acquired through taking time for myself, I honestly don't think I would have made it through that period. My retreats provided me with the opportunity to deeply contemplate my life and formulate a clear action plan to pursue my goals, both during and after those tumultuous times.

At that point in my life, I had been a part of a major global entertainment company for over three decades. However, the last five years had become increasingly unpleasant. I was not finding happiness in my work. My regular workweek extended to sixty or seventy hours, and I constantly traveled, racking up more than a hundred thousand miles a year. I was responsible for leading a team of eighteen individuals and coordinating with various external vendors. Balancing fifteen to twenty projects simultaneously became the norm. While I cherished the opportunity to work with most of the individuals on my team, I felt dissatisfied with the leadership above me within the organization.

As expected in any multinational corporation, the company's growth brought with it an increase in bureaucracy and politics. The number of individuals appointed or self-appointed as gatekeepers continued to rise, creating a complex web of overlapping and sometimes conflicting approval processes. Even obtaining approval for the most straightforward matters became a laborious task, akin to wading through bureaucratic molasses. During this time, I found myself working under my fifth management regime, reporting to two individuals. One was responsible for administrative matters, while the other, oversaw creative aspects.

The administrative manager's style often left me feeling uncertain and disconnected. There was a lack of effective communication and leadership skills such as communication, integrity, management, and others, which resulted in limited guidance and information from him.

The creative officer seemed preoccupied with his self-perceived greatness, often engaging in bad behavior that was widely known and, unfortunately, tolerated by his colleagues. It was disheartening to witness his misogynistic tendencies and bullying, which he seemed to believe were justified by his position of power.

An additional manager within the division was a third uber manager, but he seemed largely disconnected from the day-to-day affairs. His demeanor lacked any semblance of emotion or empathy toward others. The distinction between right and wrong appeared to carry the same emotional weight for him.

The stress of the situation was not good for my well-being. Maybe you or someone you know are working for one or more of these types of managers and can understand how draining that can be to one's spirit.

Over time, the happiness I once found in my job and career at this company began to fade away. Each morning, it became increasingly challenging to find motivation and navigate another workday. I found myself contemplating an exit plan, considering ways to improve my situation. It was disheartening to be in a position where I genuinely enjoyed the work I did for a company I held in high regard, yet had to endure working under managers who displayed a self-centered mindset, focused solely on managing upwards.

After enduring a prolonged period of feeling unappreciated and being subjected to disrespectful treatment, I reached a point where I realized that I needed to take charge and transform my circumstances. It became evident that nobody else was going to change my situation for me; the responsibility fell upon my shoulders. Having a supportive and competent manager would have made a world of difference. They would have provided valuable career guidance and advice, which good managers are known for.

Then, in October 2013, my older brother—my only brother—succumbed to brain cancer that was believed to have resulted from an environmental trigger during his last of three tours of duty in Afghanistan. He was 54 years old. Losing my brother at that young age made me hit the pause button on my life.

Several months before he died, I went to Maine on my annual retreat. I knew at that point that my brother's disease was terminal, that there was no cure, no reprieve—no hope. He maintained a good quality of life up until six weeks or so before he passed away when he went into home hospice care. I cannot think of anything worse than to see a loved one slowly decline in health and well-being. The brain cancer robbed him of his motor skills, with the left side of his body becoming paralyzed as the disease progressed. He fought the good fight, but ultimately, nothing could be done. I was fortunate to spend time with him at the end. It is something I will never forget.

My brother's illness made me take a serious look at my own life, my job, my career, where I wanted to be five or ten years out, and how I wanted to spend whatever remaining time I had in this world. It was a time of deep reflection on where I was and what I wanted to do. That was my first step to reassessing my entire life—not just my annual goals, but my life goals.

After my brother passed away, our father's health started a slow decline. Children are not supposed to predecease their parents. Eighteen months later, Dad passed away from what I considered to be a broken heart after losing his namesake son. A third of my family was gone in about a year and a half. It was a strain emotionally, to say the least. All that happened while I tried to hold together my personal and professional life without completely unraveling into a basket case.

I share these experiences not to evoke sympathy but to emphasize the importance of prioritizing our emotional well-being amidst life's inevitable ups and downs. My annual retreats served as a lifeline, enabling me to carefully reflect on these events and make the necessary adjustments to live a more fulfilling life during my time on this planet. Traumatic circumstances provide invaluable clarity, helping us discern what truly matters versus what does not. Whether it be loss, setbacks, or any other deeply impactful event, it is crucial to acknowledge and embrace them and allow ourselves the space for deep contemplation. This reflection becomes especially significant if we choose to reset and reorganize our priorities, focusing on what truly holds importance in our lives.

During my solo retreat to Maine in the summer of 2013, several months before my brother's death, I made the difficult decision to change careers and depart from the company. It was a challenging choice, but one that was necessary to improve my situation. Once I found solace in that realization, it became easier to plan for the changes required to create the new life I desired.

At the time, I had been steadily building a writing career, having already published several books and secured contracts for more. I found immense joy in the craft of writing and decided to take my skills to the next level by enrolling in the UCLA Writers Program. This decision was driven purely by my passion and desire to pursue something that brought me happiness while providing a means to sustain myself financially. Fortunately, I had the privilege of having a financial safety net in my savings and investments, which would support me as I embarked on building a new career. (I will delve deeper into this topic later.)

Undoubtedly, this was a significant decision that required careful consideration. I dedicated time to deep introspection, capturing my thoughts in my journal. It became evident that I was genuinely dissatisfied with my situation, and I realized that the onus was on me alone to take the necessary steps to bring about change. No one else would do it for me, nor would anyone hold my hand and guide me to the next phase of my journey. Life simply doesn't work that way. I understood that I had to initiate the change. While it was essential to plan meticulously for this transition, there came a point where I had to summon the courage to take a leap of faith and dive into the unknown. Believing in myself became paramount; I had to trust in my abilities and seize the opportunity.

It took approximately two years for me to successfully transition out of the company on my own terms. Given how the environment had deteriorated during the tenure of those managers, it wasn't overly challenging to ascertain that it was time to move on. With the assistance of an employment attorney, I was able to negotiate a favorable outcome—I left the company with the designation of retirement, accompanied by a generous compensation package and various other perks. Although bittersweet after investing almost thirty-three years in that organization, I firmly believed it was the right moment to depart.

Over time, the accumulated stress from my years of working in an untenable situation gradually dissipated. Interestingly enough, these three managers have since departed from the company.

Individuals who perpetrate negative actions eventually face the consequences of their deeds. What goes around, comes around. It is reassuring to witness that good things ultimately come to those who demonstrate patience, self-care, and compassion toward others.

Over the years, I had been developing my writing career to a point where it began to intersect with my existing job. None of these transformations associated with changing my situation and developing my writing skills would have taken place had I not taken the initiative to spend time in introspection, reflecting on my circumstances, intentions, and, most importantly, my desires. This process allowed me to establish a set of attainable goals and develop a game plan to achieve them. When confronted with challenging personalities in the workplace or life, it is essential to invest the time and patience required to consider the necessary steps and actions. Doing so empowers us to make the changes we need and want.

When I left the company in the summer of 2016, a newfound sense of vitality and freedom washed over me. It was as if a tremendous burden had been lifted from my shoulders. I didn't fully grasp it at the time, but it took a solid eighteen months to decompress from the weight of my nearly thirty-three-year tenure at that company. During that period, I established my own company to continue pursuing animation-related projects and writing, allowing me to be selective about the projects I pursued. In the following years, I received offers for positions at other companies but ultimately declined them, recognizing that they lacked the challenges or novelty I sought. I found genuine happiness in establishing myself as a writer and taking on only the work that inspired me rather than conforming to someone else's expectations. I was finally able to make choices that were truly aligned with my own best interests.

I highly doubt that I would have navigated those challenging years effectively had I not taken my annual retreats, which allowed me the precious solitude to reflect on the intricacies of my life. During those moments of quiet contemplation, I could devise a plan to change my circumstances and redirect my trajectory. I genuinely believe that everyone can benefit from periodically assessing their path and questioning whether it aligns with their true desires. If not, it becomes crucial to make the necessary adjustments and move toward what truly brings fulfillment.

For me, the most pivotal aspect of making strategic decisions was the invaluable alone time I had during those annual retreats. This time provided me with an opportunity to delve deep into my thoughts and uncover what would genuinely make me happy. I understood that no one else could embark on this introspective journey on my behalf; only I had the power to do so. If I had neglected this crucial step, I would have remained trapped in an unhappy cycle, expending energy without progressing toward any meaningful destination.

A Life You Desire to Lead

Far too often, I find myself advising friends and colleagues that mere wishes or indefinite waiting for some distant future will never pave the way to achieving our desires. Real progress can only be made through concrete goals, well-crafted plans, and taking actionable steps toward them. These tangible actions enable us to manifest the life we truly want.

To create a solid plan, it is crucial to first establish clear goals and then determine the necessary actions to achieve them. Nobody is going to guide us by the hand and lead us toward their own goals. The choice to pursue our goals lies squarely with us. Without making that choice, we would simply continue spinning in circles like a hamster on a wheel.

Lately, friends and acquaintances often express sentiments like *"I want your life," "I wish I were you,"* or *"You're living a wonderful life,"* and wonder how I manage to accomplish so much. The truth is, it all boils down to regularly assessing where you are in relation to your goals and how you are progressing toward them. When I first embarked on my journey of writing books, I dedicated significant time during my annual retreat to contemplate this idea. I recall sitting at a picnic table in a serene spot along the coast of Maine, gazing out at the water for hours, deep in thought. During that retreat, I compiled a list of book titles that came to mind. Alongside each title, I jotted down a brief one-to-two-sentence description, enough to visualize the essence of each book. Since then, I have managed to cross off most of those titles as they have been published or are on the verge of publication.

During subsequent retreats, I have continued to add more books to that list. As you achieve one goal, you always have another waiting in the wings. I firmly believe in the importance of continuously striving toward a goal. Once you accomplish one, you must promptly set new ones, ensuring that there is always a distant goal to strive for. Without such direction, you will begin to feel adrift, like a boat without a rudder. For me, having a sense of purpose is paramount. Without it, we question the contribution we are making to this world.

It is disheartening to witness individuals retire and seemingly do little more than passively watch television or attend doctors' appointments, appearing to contribute very little. After a long career of achieving goals, they suddenly come to a halt in retirement, engaging in inactivity. Sadly, more often than not, within a year or two, they pass away. I vividly recall two artists I knew who had devoted over fifty and fifty-four years to the company, respectively. Shortly after retiring, both of them passed away within a year.

Conversely, those who maintain a sense of purpose, set new goals, and continue to contribute in different ways, whether through a new career path, volunteering, or any number of endeavors, seem to thrive. I have witnessed my sister, who worked at a financial firm in New York for many years, where the founder continued to work and make meaningful contributions well beyond retirement age. In fact, on his 102nd birthday, while the employees threw a party for him, he requested that they celebrate every other birthday from then on. Remarkably, he lived to be over 106 years old. The key lies in staying active, engaged, and striving toward goals.

It is important to recognize that retirement should not mark the end of one's engagement with life but rather an opportunity to redirect energy toward new endeavors and continued personal growth. By maintaining an active and purposeful lifestyle, we can experience fulfillment and vitality well beyond the traditional retirement age.

Everything I have accomplished and continue to pursue is a result of the consistent practice of setting short-and-long-term goals during my retreats. These goals undergo regular review and adjustment throughout the year. Anyone and everyone can adopt this practice during their own retreats, regardless of the amount of time available. It has become a deeply ingrained habit in my life, an integral part of who I am, and something I conscientiously schedule each year. Not taking this dedicated time for myself or claiming that I don't have the time is simply not an option for me, and it should not be for you, either.

Consider taking a moment to track your daily routine. How much time do you spend in front of the television, engrossed in your smartphone, or stuck in traffic? What excuses do you find yourself using to justify not having time for certain things or claiming to be too busy? The reality is that we have complete control over every waking moment of our day, and it is up to us to decide how we use that time. Breaking free from old habits and putting in the effort required to bring about changes in our lives can be challenging. It involves hard work. However, only you can take that step if you genuinely desire it. You can continue to postpone it until tomorrow, or you can choose to make it happen today. The decision of whether to commit to the work needed to achieve your desires, your goals, lies solely with you. Going on a personal retreat will assist you in focusing your attention on making the choices that align with what you truly want.

Over the years, I have observed a prevalent trend in which many individuals give up when they realize that achieving something requires hard work. Our society is driven by instant gratification, where many seek immediate satisfaction through consumerism, buying things they truly don't need, or searching for the easy way out—a so-called shortcut. However, greatness and attaining what you truly desire do not come through shortcuts. They demand dedicated effort and hard work. If one is unwilling to put in the necessary work to reach their goals and dreams, then perhaps those goals were not truly worthwhile from the start, or they simply gave up before exerting the effort required to attain them.

Throughout my experiences in countless creative classes—be it painting, sculpture, or writing—I have witnessed individuals investing their hard-earned money only to abandon their pursuits after a mere couple of sessions into the semester. Once they realized that artmaking or writing entailed substantial effort and the creation of something from nothing, they became disheartened and quit. They had mistakenly believed that taking a few classes would automatically lead to publishing their work or selling their masterpieces. However, life does not operate in such a manner. While there may be exceptions, for the most part, one must put in a genuine effort to achieve their goals and aspirations.

It is essential to recognize that you cannot simply coast your way to success or expect it to be handed to you without paying your dues. Every individual who has attained significant success has done so by investing considerable effort and perseverance. They had clear goals and a well-defined plan to achieve those goals.

My journey of personal retreats began long before I encountered the challenging years of family tragedy and loss. It served me well during the good times, preparing me to navigate the difficult periods. I dedicated myself to developing an annual personal retreat, investing unwavering commitment, discipline, and effort. The rewards were significant, and I believe you, too, can experience the same if you are willing to make a similar investment.

The truth is, there are no shortcuts to constructing the life you genuinely desire to lead. It involves setting goals, visualizing them, and diligently working toward them. I have come to understand that obtaining what I want is all about crafting a well-thought-out plan, staying focused on it, and making adjustments along the way to ensure I stay on course until I reach the desired outcome. Once achieved, I move forward to my next goal, repeating the process. The purpose of *Find Your Happy Place: The 8-Step Guide to Boosting Your Creativity through a Personal Retreat* is precisely to assist you in organizing your own personal solo retreat and establishing it as an annual habit. By doing so, you can pave the way to lead the life you genuinely aspire to live.

Find Your Happy Place: The 8-Step Guide to Boosting Your Creativity through a Personal Retreat is based on my over thirty years of personal retreats and annual self-assessments. The process I have distilled into this guide will bring clarity, focus, and renewal that will energize you for the year ahead if you are honest with yourself and work at your own self-improvement. It will rejuvenate your body, mind, and spirit, allowing you to get the most out of the life you want to lead.

If you follow the very simple steps in this book, you'll see your life change in a positive way, as it did for me. By setting bold goals and following through on achieving them, you will increase your chances of success by understanding what it looks like to you. When you take the steps to break up your big goals into smaller chunks and accomplish those in a logical order, you will be able to track your performance. At the same time, you can celebrate each milestone toward the greater goal. Doing so will put you into a unique group of purpose-oriented individuals who have taken charge of their lives, broken from the pack, and achieved their goals. They have found their happy place, and the only question is, will you *Find Your Happy Place?!*

— *My Annual Retreat* —

I set up my red, lightweight, foldable camping chair on the edge of a dew-covered lawn, just outside the shade of a gnarled crabapple tree growing off an embankment that drops to the shoreline below. The morning sun illuminates the boats moored in the cove; their reflections shimmer on the water's surface. Flags atop the century-old boathouse nearby flap to the benevolent breeze coming off the ocean. I adjust the chair a few times to have the perfect view before sitting down to soak up the warm sun rays, my legs crossed, my feet resting on a weathered wooden fence rail that serves as my ottoman on the slope's edge.

As the day heats up, I can smell the scent of freshly cut grass mixed with the salt air. It is a mainstay of summer. I hear the chirping birds and the intermittent buzzing of cicadas and watch a bald eagle swoop down to pluck a fish from the water. Bees zip around a cluster of wildflowers, and butterflies feast on a milkweed plant, battling the light air coming off Eggemoggin Reach just beyond the cove. The muted clanging of halyards on sailboat masts sounds like church bells in the distance on a lazy Sunday morning.

The clacking of a diesel engine breaks the sound of the natural world. A lobster boat motors along in the distance as a white wake rolls out behind the vessel. I take in a deep breath of sea air, clean and crisp. I exhale with a smile and look around momentarily to make sure no one else has found this idyllic, secluded spot. They never have, but as a nervous habit, I check anyway. I begin to feel the weight of everyday stress drain from my shoulders. I am finally alone in my thoughts.

White clouds drift across the indigo sky, and for a few hours, time stands still. I go deep into thought, and in a flash, three or four hours have vanished. I just sit there in solitude and stillness, in my own contemplation, occasionally moving my chair into the shade of the tree canopy. This is my happy place, away from everything and everyone, where I make a pilgrimage annually to be in my thoughts without the distractions of the everyday world—alone in nature. I review the year gone by and plan for the new one ahead with enthusiasm and positivity. I'm on my own personal retreat.

Now, my happy place and your happy place may be the same or completely different, but the important thing is that you find that place. That one spot where you can be away from everything and everybody. The place that will allow you to leave behind your self-consciousness and the influences of others and allow you to focus solely on yourself.

Have you ever thought about the last time you were able to take time just for yourself? Some people might think about a time when they were able to steal an hour to walk alone on a beach or go on a hike in the woods before meeting up with someone. Just take a moment and think back to when you took a block of time just for yourself alone. It may be hard for you to remember a specific time. Don't be surprised; many people cannot think of one either.

In today's fast-paced world, too often, people find it hard to spend time truly alone and away from their normal daily workday and family routine. Even sitting and reading a book or the paper on a weekend morning in the backyard or on the balcony still isn't much alone time. There is always a smartphone buzzing with emails and calls, a knock at the door, or any number of interruptions. How about when you take a vacation? Even if you went on one alone, you are likely sightseeing and interacting with those around you on a tour, in a café, or just strolling through a shopping district. We're never really alone unless we make a conscious effort to do so.

Friends and colleagues have been genuinely fascinated by the fact that I take an annual retreat every summer for several weeks as a way to refresh, recharge, and refocus my life. It is my time—me time— for introspection, meditation, and setting and evaluating my intentions and life goals. This is where I can be in my own thoughts, uninterrupted, in another place that allows me to break the bonds of my daily routines. A place where I can reflect on the past year's successes and the occasional lack of success and look to the future with confidence. This solo retreat allows me to be immersed in an environment, alone in nature, where I can actually think with minimal distractions.

Over many decades, I have developed a process for my private retreat that has had positive, life-altering benefits. I believe this process will also offer the same effect in reaching your goals if you are serious about changing your situation.

Yes, we all have to have goals. They are part of who we are and what we want to accomplish. It's our ambition, whether great or small. Goals reflect our desires to make the most of life and to contribute to creating happiness not just for ourselves but for our loved ones and those around us in our daily world. Author and motivational speaker Zig Ziglar says, "Goals enable you to do more for yourself and others, too."[1] Goals are essentially a roadmap to your life. Without goals, how do you know where you are going? Goals are a destination, and reaching them is our journey.

Using your retreat to review past goals and set new ones is an important part of *Find Your Happy Place: The 8-Step Guide to Boosting Your Creativity through a Personal Retreat*. It is your game plan for life. The common denominator for everyone is the desire to lead a fulfilling life and ultimately be happy in who we are and what we do with that life.

If you find that you are not happy with where you are, change your course and drive toward the life that will make you fulfilled and happy. Yes, I have found that it is that simple. Yet, I have seen many never take the time to think about where they are now and where they are going in their own personal fulfillment.

Like many others, I used to accept my current situation as predetermined or somehow my destiny and was not motivated to change. But then I realized I had the power to change my situation if I wanted to. I could either sit there and accept where I was and what I was in life or set about to make positive changes. It was all up to me.

No one would do it for me. I had to do it for myself, and I will tell you throughout this book that I did it because I could. I took charge of my situations by making small and sometimes large changes in each instance, which have since paid dividends beyond my wildest imaginations. The choice is up to you—to all of us— to make our lives all they can be. *Find Your Happy Place* and setting goals to do the necessary work on a personal retreat will help you achieve the things in life that will make you joyful.

I found my happy place long ago and return to it annually. Every year, like clockwork, I head up to a small coastal town in northern Maine. There is a seasonal school there that specializes in boatbuilding and related arts where I will take a class in something I've never done before. One year, I learned how to make a pair of oars; another year, I learned how to carve signs in wood. I spent several years rediscovering my love of dimensional art by creating wildlife sculptures that I continue to make to this day. Following that week of class, I take a week for myself. A totally unscheduled week that allows me to do anything I want or nothing at all. Maine is a place where I can learn something new, unplug if I want to, and simply be alone in my thoughts. It is my happy place. What is yours?

Have you ever just sat in your own thoughts for hours uninterrupted? Truly sat alone without your phone buzzing or the television on or someone interrupting you to ask for something? By going off to a different or new place, you can achieve a peaceful, meditative state that will allow you to be in your own thoughts, examine the past year of achievements, and project what you wish to accomplish in the coming year. This is a time to reconnect with yourself, refresh, recharge, and reset.

Over the years, I've learned that creating your personal retreat must be carefully considered and planned in advance. You have to carve out the time, whether a few hours, a day, a week, or longer. You can do this once you understand the importance of taking time for yourself. The idea is to create a solo retreat for yourself—only yourself.

Bill Gates, the co-founder of Microsoft, calls his personal retreat his "Think Week." He takes seven days a year and goes off by himself—no family, friends, or staff—to read and think. The only exception is a caretaker who slips him two meals a day. Gates spends the time contemplating the future, which is his way of thinking about new ideas. He goes to a small lake house in a forest with a stack of reading material. The house has a plain desk in front of a window with a view of the lake, a wall lined with books, and a refrigerator stocked with beverages. Out of this annual think week, he was inspired to write his famous "The Internet Tidal Wave[2]" memo to the executive staff at Microsoft and came up with the plan for the Microsoft Tablet PC, among many other ideas. That week lets Gates think about the future of technology and how he wants to tackle issues facing his company and, through his foundation, humanity[3].

Not everyone can take a full week off for a personal retreat, but it is something we can strive for if we truly want to make productive changes in our own lives. Finding your happy place once a year will help you gain perspective and map out your route for the future. It can help you refocus on those things that are important to you and take the long view for the year ahead.

Too often, we focus on instant gratification without thinking about the consequences of those choices on the future. Sometimes, short-term gains take away from the long-term goal, pushing it further out of reach. These are things you should think about on your personal retreat, which will help you focus on what truly matters.

A personal retreat can also help to provide discipline to your life since you're forced to stop, reflect, think clearly, and make more rational decisions. Not making a snap decision gives us the power to decide what is right for us and not go along with the hot new trend or what is "cool" just because everyone else is doing it. You have to learn to think through your choices and decide their impact on your goals.

An annual solo retreat prevents inaction and stagnation in our lives. By setting goals for the coming year, we are putting into motion a plan with an achievable outcome. You will be able to review and tweak your plan as the year progresses, and it will aid you in making smart choices on a daily, weekly, and monthly basis. The key component to reaching your ultimate goal is evaluating each decision you make concerning the individual steps needed to achieve that goal.

But, taking a solo retreat is not just about goals. It is also about mind, body, and spirit— taking time to reflect, refresh, unplug, and recharge is critical for our mental, physical, and psychological well-being.[4] It is about taking time to examine ourselves both inwardly and outwardly, our emotions and our character. Examining and thinking about our emotional well-being and moral beliefs is important to keeping ourselves centered.

What about your personal relationships— are you unhappy with your partner or wish you had one? I believe that taking time for yourself each year is healthy for any relationship, whether you are with a spouse, partner, friend, or co-worker. Time away from these relationships actually helps to strengthen bonds and lets you see these individuals in a different light. There is truth to the old adage, "Absence makes the heart grow fonder." Spending time thinking about loved ones allows you to put relationships in perspective, understand other viewpoints, and gain greater empathy.

In your job or career path, it may be about questioning where you are and where you want to go. Are you happy with your chosen profession and the company you work for? Do you feel like your company has moral values, or are you trapped in a dead-end position? Is your boss fair and decent or not a good person? If you are unhappy with the job, career, company, or boss, what do you want to do to change that? How do you feel? How do you look? What are your dreams and desires, and how will you achieve them in relation to your profession? These are issues that sometimes don't have simple or clear answers. These topics require deep thought far out of range of distractions, and where you can also develop an action plan to change if that's what *you* want to do.

These are all questions you should ask yourself regularly if you're going to lead the life you want and accomplish all the things you dream about. If you don't do that, you may be making haphazard choices that will not serve you well in the long run. Don't go along with the crowd or be shortsighted—shortchanging yourself and what you can get out of life.

This is not mumbo-jumbo; this is how successful people— not just celebrities or well-known entrepreneurs, but regular people like you and me— manage their lives and reach their goals. That is why, after decades of taking my own personal retreats, I have written down what I have learned. It has worked for me for many years and can work for you if you want to change.

When people take an interest in learning more about my personal retreat, some express curiosity, others skepticism, even envy, but mostly, they want to learn how to take their own personal retreat. They want to understand how to do it so they get the most out of their own time alone.

It's not hard; it's not rocket science. Like anything else, it's a learned skill, and I know from experience that creating a personal retreat can have a profound, transformative impact on your life. You can do this, the exact same thing I've done for decades, once you know how to develop the skills and discipline to make *Find Your Happy Place* a part of your life.

— *Step 1* —

HOW MUCH TIME AND WHEN TO TAKE IT

Above all else, the first step in this journey is to decide when you want to take your personal retreat and for how long. This choice is likely to hinge on your work commitments. If you are an educator, selecting the summer months between school years may be best. Alternatively, various professions might offer a natural lull period, presenting an opportune moment to plan your time off, or the seasons themselves might dictate the ideal timeframe. It is plausible that you are employed in a seasonal field, where either summer or winter corresponds to the busiest periods. The key here is to pick a time that harmonizes most effectively with both your personal and professional life.

There is no point in taking some time off if you are going to be badgered by pressing family or work-related matters. So, choose the time wisely. I typically take my solo retreat sometime between late July and Labor Day weekend in early September. Anytime during the month of August is usually a good time as my world slows down, and many colleagues take vacations then. That seems to work best for me consistently year in and year out. What will work best for you year over year?

Once you have decided when you can take the time off, you will have to determine how much time you can take for yourself. You may only be able to get a weekend or one day, which is still better than nothing. The important part here is that you give yourself as much time as possible to relax your mind and body.

I was fortunate in that when I started my personal retreats, I was able to take a full week. My wife was open and encouraged me to do it. After that first retreat, when I realized how rejuvenating it was and how refreshed I felt when I returned, I knew I had to repeat it.

The following year, I did it again and then continued to take a week each year for the next decade. Then, I expanded my retreat to two weeks, and for a number of years, I even did three weeks. Okay, three weeks was a bit much— even my wife thought that was too long to be away.

It was all about trial and error in those early years as I developed, experimented, and refined my retreat process. I understand that taking weeks off might not be possible, but you have to find the right amount of time that works for you. You might try something new each year to avoid falling into a routine other than taking a personal retreat. That is why my retreat grew from a week to two weeks to three weeks, then back down to two weeks, which is the sweet spot for me.

Yes, three weeks was a long time. Those three-week retreats were during some difficult years in my personal and professional life when my brother and father died, and I was dealing with the unpleasant managers. I was grateful to be able to take that time then, as it made an enormous difference in my life today. But the solo retreat at two weeks feels perfect. It allows me to take a weeklong class of some sort and then follow it with a week of reading, writing, and meditating—being in my own thoughts.

The class I take in the first week is usually something I have never done before or something that requires full concentration on my part. This serves two distinct purposes. First, it allows me to gradually wind down from my normal family and work life. That means unplugging by disconnecting from all the devices for the most part and letting people know I'll have limited access to my phone and emails. It is also about changing the daily routine. At home, I tend to start my day early by going through emails, and then I go to a local Starbucks for tea before heading to my office to begin my workday.

On my retreat, I still wake early, but I may read a book I brought before having a light breakfast and heading to a class that first week. It is not a drastically different routine but rather a relaxed one that allows me to ease into the retreat. A different daily structure helps in the winding down process from my regular work and family life, which is important to the success of the overall retreat.

That is what works for me. What amount of time works for you? It may take you several retreats to figure that out. There is no set rule to how much or how little time you take; it should only be the right amount of time that works for you without the influence of other's opinions. It is the quality of that time that matters most. Only you can decide the sweet spot to get the most out of your personal retreat.

Remember, this is solo time for yourself. You don't take this retreat with a spouse or a friend; that defeats the purpose. That also goes for trying to do a structured retreat at a spa; it misses the point of being completely alone in your thoughts without distractions.

You also want to think about an environment where you want to be alone. I go to such a sparsely populated area of Maine that there is little in the way of retail conveniences. The nearest coffee shop is at least twenty to thirty minutes away. This is one of the reasons I enjoy going to this spot on the coast of Maine— it is rural and completely different from my everyday environment. There are fewer distractions. My regular home-work environment is so common that half the time, I am on autopilot when I run errands or go to an appointment. But even though I have been on my retreat to Maine many times before, everything still feels fresh since I only visit there once a year. I notice the little things like the bald eagles flying around, the trees, wild turkeys running in a field, the smell of fresh wildflowers, and the clean sea air. I can take note of the wind patterns moving across the water's surface in the cove, how the clouds drift across the cerulean blue sky, and how the lupines dance in an afternoon breeze. That is one of the benefits of going to a different locale than you are used to. It allows you to *see* the world around you with all your senses.

It also helps to clear my mind of work and real-life related thoughts so I can concentrate on learning a new skill by working with hand or power tools that require complete focus lest I lose a finger. Not only am I focused on learning a new skill, but I am going at my own pace. I don't feel rushed, and I purposefully take my time on each step of the process to learn it before moving on to the next step. I am in the class eight hours a day for five days or sometimes six days, depending on the curriculum of the particular class. I will go into more depth on the different types of classes available in Step 2.

During the week that I am taking a class, I tend to go to bed early each evening, typically at 8:30 or 9:00 PM. That allows me to get a deep sleep of seven to eight hours, which is healthy for both mind and body. Sleep restores and repairs our body on the cellular level. Not getting enough sleep can profoundly impact your health and affect how you think, work, learn, react, and generally get along with those around you. Getting enough sleep helps our brain function properly, improving our ability to learn. Sleep plays a role in how well we pay attention, make decisions, and how creative we are during our waking hours.

Chances are that you are not getting enough sleep during your regular work week. The retreat can give you a refresher on how well you can function with a restful, deep sleep. Sleep is part of good health and supports a healthy immune system. Getting the right amount of sleep influences how our body reacts to hormones like insulin, which controls our blood sugar levels[5]. Not getting enough sleep can increase the risk of type 2 diabetes and other illnesses.[6] Being on your personal retreat will allow you to plan for a deep sleep just by retiring early without interruption.

The other thing I like about where I take my retreat is that there is no television, electronic gadgets, or newspapers; for the most part, I can completely unplug. I tend to read and reflect during the off-hours from class. This is part of preparing for the following week of deep thought, meditation, and journaling alone. The reading material is tailored to what I am interested in thinking about while on the retreat. It may be directly or indirectly related to specific intentions, goals, or issues I want to meditate on. I bring hard copies of books, articles, and other material I want to read and shy away from reading them on a device screen as a way of really unplugging.

Okay, I do have a cell phone with me, and I do check my emails once in the evening while having dinner, and I do call my wife to check in with her each day. But that is me. That works for me, and it may not work for you. That is the point of a solo retreat— you must design it to work for you. This is not a one-size-fits-all type of program. The point of designing your retreat is that it is your *customized* time away. You can scale any of this to work for your own time. You may want to take a day or two to wind down and relax instead of an entire week. This is your time to figure out what will work for you and no one else. Each of us has our own happy place, that special place we enjoy visiting, and we will know it when we experience it. I promise you that.

By the end of that first week, I am more relaxed and rested which then sets me up for the second week of the solo retreat. That second half of the retreat is the most important part— it's where I can sink into a more thoughtful, meditative state of mind. This portion of the retreat is the most productive in reviewing the past year and projecting forward intentions and goals for the next twelve months. This is where the real work gets done for me.

Once you have decided on how much time to devote to your retreat, you will need to pick the dates. It's not just about how long you'll be away but also when you'll go and how far out you plan the retreat. To me, this is as important as the length of time and place. I tend to pick my dates in December for the following year and block them out on my calendar. That means that often I am making my arrangements eight to nine months in advance.

You may decide, based on your budget and the time you've allotted to your retreat, that you will want to drive or bike to the location, but it is still important to make all your arrangements well in advance. You may need to scope out a quiet location at a park, get a parking permit, make other reservations, or pay fees in advance. There may even be an opportunity to pre-order a picnic lunch from a local eatery for each day you take your retreat. That way, when you are in a quiet, safe place, you can have lunch when you want to without having to go someplace, keeping you in the mindfulness of the moment.

Mindfulness is the practice of paying attention in the moment without judgment. It is a meditation practice that refers to the deliberate act of regulating your attention by observing your thoughts, emotions, and the state of your body. It is the "quality or state of being conscious or aware of something."[7] That something is your intention, your goal, or an issue of importance to you.

For at least the last fifty years, clinical psychologists and psychiatrists have used mindfulness to treat and reduce the symptoms of anxiety, stress, drug addiction, and varying degrees of depression. Mindfulness programs have been employed to aid in weight loss and management, senior health, athletic performance, and prisoner rehabilitation.[8] Countless studies point to the positive effects of using mindfulness techniques as a "preventive strategy to halt the development of mental-health problems.[9]"

Once I have the dates on my calendar, I make it immovable, barring any emergency. On the first week of January every year, right after New Year's Day, usually the first business day of the new year, I book my plane tickets, register for the class I will be taking, and reserve my accommodations. I get a great price on the airline tickets and lock in where I will stay, which has become the same place every year. It also makes the dates permanent on my calendar since I have already paid for much of the retreat in advance to get the best prices. That makes it more difficult to move or cancel since that involves change fees. It also forces others to modify their plans if they want me to attend a meeting or other work or family-related matter. If something falls within my retreat, I just decline it since I already have my retreat set in stone.

Blocking out the dates on the calendar and then letting your loved ones and others know in advance will avoid any possible issues. I advise discussing the retreat first and preparing your significant other for your plans. My wife never had an issue with me taking these personal retreats, but I know some might. I have had guys say to me from the start, "Man, how does your wife let you do that; mine would never!" or a woman remark, "My husband would have a real issue with that." I think one of the most important aspects of a relationship is trust. You either have it or you don't. If trust is an issue, you may want to work on improving your relationship.

I tend not only to discuss my plans with my family when I make all the arrangements, but I also periodically remind my wife, family, and friends several times in the months leading up to the actual retreat. This will prevent anyone from being surprised or not remembering that you had told them months ago about your retreat. Reminding the relevant people about your retreat via email or sending a calendar invite may be useful.

In the early years of my personal retreats, I did not discuss it with anyone outside my family. It was a personal thing I wanted to keep private. Over time, enough people started to become curious since I took the time off by myself each year, and I began to speak about it to close friends, eventually widening that circle. It was my time, and these people respected that. Whether you want to discuss it or not is your option; only you can determine the right way to handle it.

Remember that once you have set the dates for your

personal retreat, do your best to set them in stone. Make those dates immovable; it's your time. It is your retreat, and it should be handled the way you would a health issue since this is all about your mental and physical well-being.

Quick Tips:

1. Determine the right amount of time for your personal retreat.
2. Determine when best to take that time for your personal retreat.

Worksheet:
How Much Time and When to Take a Personal Retreat

Part 1: Assessing Your Time

1. How much vacation time do you have available to use for a personal retreat?

   _____

   _____

2. Are there any upcoming work or personal commitments that may interfere with taking a personal retreat?

   _____

   _____

   _____

   _____

3. How much time can you realistically dedicate to a personal retreat without compromising your other responsibilities?

_____

_____

Part 2: Determining When to Take Your Retreat

1. When is the best time of year for you to take a personal retreat? Consider factors such as weather, work demands, and family commitments.

_____

_____

_____

2. How much advance notice do you need to provide your employer, clients, or family members before taking a personal retreat?

_____

_____

_____

_____

_____

_____

3. Are there any major events or projects coming up in your personal or professional life that may affect when you can take a personal retreat?

_____

_____

_____

_____

_____

_____

_____

Part 3: Planning Your Retreat Length

1. How long do you want your personal retreat to be?

_____

_____

2. Can you realistically take off that amount of time from work and other responsibilities?

_____

_____

3. If you can't take off the entire length of time you want, could you take a shorter retreat instead?

_____

_____

Part 4: Making the Most of Your Retreat

1. What specific goals or intentions do you have for your personal retreat?

_____

_____

_____

_____

_____

_____

2. What activities or practices will you engage in during your retreat to support your goals and intentions?

_____

_____

_____

_____

3. How will you follow through on your insights and intentions gained during the retreat once you return to your normal routine?

_____

_____

_____

_____

Part 5: Reflection

1. After taking your personal retreat, reflect on the length of time you took and the timing of the retreat. Did it feel like enough time? Was the timing right for you?

_____

_____

2. Reflect on your goals and intentions. Were they realistic? Did you achieve what you wanted to achieve during your retreat?

_____

_____

_____

_____

_____

_____

3. Finally, consider whether you would take a personal retreat again, and if so, what you would do differently next time.

_____

_____

_____

_____

_____

_____

— ✑ —

Remember, taking a personal retreat is a personal decision and should be based on your individual needs and circumstances. Use this worksheet as a guide to help you determine the best length of time and timing for your personal retreat.

— *Step 2* —

WHERE TO TAKE YOUR RETREAT

With the duration and timing of your retreat determined, the next step is to deliberate upon the destination. It is possible that you already have a clear idea of where you wish to go, as you may have a cherished setting in mind - a personal sanctuary that never fails to evoke joy and contentment whenever you find yourself there. This "happy place" of yours holds a special significance, and selecting it as your retreat location would be an intuitive choice. On the other hand, if you have yet to pinpoint that perfect spot, you may find yourself engaged in the task of exploring various options and contemplating where this extraordinary place could be.

Some people like the beach, others the mountains. Some people like a lake district, and some prefer the desert or a rural farming area. If all you can take off is one day, a local park will suffice. Regardless of your time and location limitations, there are still plenty of options to take your tailored retreat in a location that will afford some privacy and seclusion.

There is no shortage of options for a personal retreat, and you will have to determine what level of seclusion works best for you. There is a home on top of a tower deep in the Oregon wilderness that doesn't have any frills— no television, no Wi-Fi, there isn't even a clock. The bathroom is an outhouse four flights of stairs down from the house. The nearest grocery store or gas station is an hour away, and it rents for $200 a night.[10] That might be perfect for some but too remote for others. The where for your retreat will no doubt have to fit within your comfort zone and, of course, your budget. A small rural town may be more to your liking, a place where you can walk to a general store or café and have a little human interaction but still spend time by yourself undisturbed.

I stay in a boarding house that includes three meals a day of homecooked food, which works out to be very inexpensive. I get a hot breakfast, a sandwich lunch, and a hot dinner in the evening. The food is very fresh and prepared homestyle, and you have as much or as little as you like.

My spartan room is ten by twelve feet with a single twin bed, a nightstand, a lamp, a dresser, a small chair, and a wall-mounted rack for hanging clothes. There is no closet. The shared bathroom is down the hall. In the more than thirty years I've stayed there, I have never had a room key or locked my door. On warm days, I have often left my door open so the air can circulate. And no, I have never had anything taken or gone missing. The monk-like accommodations are austere but very pleasant at the same time, and that in and of itself is refreshing.

I can go for days without spending any money out of pocket because there aren't many retail establishments. There is a local general store that has been in continuous operation since 1857 that I can walk to for a newspaper or a beverage during the day. I rarely do, but it's there if I want it. I can drive to a town twenty minutes away that has a few restaurants and shops, which allows me to have some choices if I decide to do something different on the spur of the moment, like getting an ice cream cone one afternoon. It's all about what works for you. This place has worked for me for decades with little change during that time.

It may be hard to believe, but there are still places where you can go that are completely safe. Where people are respectful of one another's belongings, and you can leave your doors unlocked or the keys in the car without worrying. These places still exist and make you feel as though you are stepping back in time to a different era and way of life.

However, I recommend getting to know an area well before you feel comfortable enough to leave the doors unlocked or keys in the ignition.

One of the factors that will contribute to your choice of location is whether you will want to sign up for a class or some sort of educational experience. A simple online search will yield a tremendous selection of courses across the nation and around the world. Take a moment to think about something you always wanted to learn or try, and then search online to see what is available. Maybe you have always wanted to try photography[11]; there are plenty of one- and two-day or even weeklong classes taught by professionals. There are painting classes[12], book bindery[13], writing[14], boat building[15], sculpture[16], woodworking[17], and more that span skill levels from beginner to advanced. These classes, offered throughout the year or seasonally, are enriching ways to begin a personal retreat.

Have you ever thought about taking archery lessons[18] or learning how to sail[19] or quilt[20]? Maybe you always wanted to make and bottle your own beer or wine. There are classes for nearly everything you can think of, and there is no time better in your life than now to learn something new. There are weeklong classes where you can build your own kayak[21] near Seattle, Washington, on the Chesapeake Bay in Maryland, or in various spots throughout New England. You can take one-, two-, or four-day classes in basket weaving[22] in Minnesota or Massachusetts. There is a woodcut printing[23] class in Florida. If there is something you want to try, there is probably a class for it near you or within a region of the country you would like to go to for your retreat. Become a life-long learner and enjoy the benefits that acquiring a new skill plays in your life and in increasing your creativity. This is a great way to get your creative juices flowing before spending time alone in deep thought.

I like being able to sit near a small cove where I can hear the water lapping against the shoreline, the clanging of halyards on the masts of moored sailboats, and the cry of seagulls gliding on the soft, gentle sea breeze. There are a number of seasonal schools in the area that offer weeklong class experiences, and some of the courses change annually, so there is always something new and interesting to learn.

Haystack Mountain School of Crafts[24] on Deer Isle, Maine, offers core summer workshops that include one- and two-week sessions in blacksmithing, clay, ceramics, fiber, glass, graphics, metals, and wood. You could learn chair making at The Center for Furniture Craftsmanship[25] in Rockport, Maine, where they have classes on fine furniture making. Thousands of classes are offered through small specialty schools nationwide, and many are reasonably priced.

You should also note that plenty of one-and two-day classes are offered on weekends. So, even if you have limited time, you can still take a short class at a local school or community college. Many universities and colleges offer one-day workshops on weekends on any number of topics. If all you have is a weekend, you can take a one-day class and then take another day or two to be someplace secluded where you can be in your thoughts and set some goals. The personal retreat is yours to design how you want.

You will find that learning one new skill will pay dividends in not just how you look at your job but in allowing you to "see" things in a different way. What I mean by "see" things differently is that you will be enlightened by the knowledge that you pick up from learning a new skill and how it will relate to other aspects of your life.

Whether you take a class or not, the next part of the retreat is being out in nature. This is especially important if you are a city dweller and is highly recommended for your solo retreat. Nature has restorative and rejuvenating qualities that stimulate all your senses.

Taking a long walk in the woods or hiking on a trail in a National Park as the leaves rustle on the trees while breathing in clean air is refreshing and will make you feel alive again. The movement and increase in oxygen will stimulate your brain. Walking on a beach or shoreline in solitude with the breeze coming off the water is soul-cleansing. Hearing the ocean surf crashing against the coast and the wind in the dunes and feeling the sun's warmth on your face may bring you intense joy. Getting out into nature, moving about, and taking deep breaths of fresh air can make you feel clearheaded, renewed, recharged, and primed for deep thinking or meditation.

The place you chose is for you and only you, where you can slip into solitude, plan, and create the life you want to lead. It is important for you to think in terms of *your* life. This is a fluid process and one you have to tailor for yourself. As I have mentioned earlier, there is no one-size-fits-all retreat; each is and must be different because we are all unique and different.

I have been doing my personal retreat for so long that it is a nearly automatic process for me to plan. There is a "footprint" already in place, and I know that the day after New Year's Day, I will be making the arrangements for my retreat later in the year. That includes setting my goals, which I'll discuss in detail in the next chapter. This customized process you will learn to create incorporates some basic steps around goal creation, action plans, and what to do once you reach a goal.

The retreat is a process you must start and plan in solitude without distractions and outside influences. A retreat is best done in nature while you think unabated and undisturbed. Outside of taking a class, it is not something that is preplanned through a series of activities that are scheduled throughout the day. A *Find Your Happy Place* retreat doesn't involve joint exercises, "trust falls," or interacting with others in some pre-planned, structured activities.

I want to caution you not to be tempted by a resort that advertises structured retreats. As I write this book, I am seeing more of these services being offered by hotels. Kudos to the resort operators for experimenting and trying new things, but going to a resort to take a solo retreat is like trying to read a book at a NASCAR race. There are just too many diversions and too much noise, not to mention the structured activities that the resort's "cruise directors" have planned, all of which will keep you from accomplishing the deep thinking your personal retreat is designed to give you. These types of "retreats" fill your day with organized group activities that cost a lot of money. They defeat the purpose of a solo retreat. Let's call them what they truly are: spa weekends or packages that are great for relaxing but not for deep thinking, introspection, and reflecting.

And please don't confuse the solo retreat with going on a family vacation to an all-inclusive resort. A solo retreat to find your happy place is not a vacation you want to take with family, friends, or loved ones. The emphasis is on *solo*—by yourself, in seclusion or near seclusion for deep thought immersion into your dreams, goals, and life path. You must do this on your own without the input of others to taint your desires. It is a "no group-think zone" but rather a place where you can sit, undisturbed, in stillness for hours if you want.

Sitting in stillness, aware of your state of being—mindfulness—gives you the improved ability to pay attention, focus, and concentrate on one topic, problem, or desire. The act of sitting in stillness, aware of your thoughts, emotions, body, and breathing, will reduce your stress levels, increase your capacity to overcome challenges, and expand your creativity through the use of your imagination. Author Pico Iyer wrote in *The Art of Stillness*, "It's easy to feel as if we're standing two inches away from a huge canvas that's noisy and crowded and changing with every microsecond. It's only by stepping farther back and standing still that we can begin to see what that canvas (which is our life) really means, and to take in the larger picture."[26] The seclusion that a remote place offers allows us to step away from the hustle and bustle of the normal world, "the canvas," and to see what is truly important to each of us.

Being in a present moment of awareness gives you clarity of mind and the ability to concentrate on one immediate thing, which could be an intention, goal, relationship, or problem you are trying to solve. It allows you to see clearly and analyze whatever you are focused on at that moment and to do so in a near blissful state. I have found that getting into a state of mindfulness enhances my ability to visualize through my imagination, which, at times, puts me into a heightened state of euphoria. This is why you want to choose the location for your personal retreat carefully and why a nature setting works so well.

It is crucial to get away from diversions and interruptions if you want to go into deep thought without hindrances or interferences. You must be able to sit with your thoughts, which can and will likely be emotional. You need to be able to cry without embarrassment or laugh out loud without receiving judgmental looks or being asked if you are okay. I cannot stress enough the importance of sitting uninhibited for hours just thinking, letting your mind wander where it will. Take a mid-day nap or read on and off. The key is to think, think, and think deeply.

You will be amazed at the meditative state you will experience when you are in the right environment and frame of mind. The ability to fully immerse yourself in your thoughts, imagination, and daydreams, whether logical, illogical, crazy, fanciful, or absurd, is mind-expanding and exhilarating. Some call it "zoning out" or "being in the zone." Whatever you want to call it, I can tell you from personal experience it is euphoric. I find it similar to the state of mind I often achieve when I am writing or creating art for hours.

Wherever you decide to go, I recommend bringing some good, inspirational reading material. In keeping with the idea of unplugging, I recommend physical reading materials rather than an e-reader. Bring a book you have been wanting to read or print out some articles or essays that may be inspiring to you as you begin the process of your retreat and deep thought for hours. You can read some of the material at the beginning or end of your day. If some of your reading material is related to a desire you have, then all the better for inspiring your thought process and getting your creative juices flowing. It is important to write down or highlight quotes or passages that move and inspire you. You can refer back to these for inspiration in the days and months following your personal retreat.

Quick Tips:

1. You may already know where you want to take your personal retreat and that's great. You are one step ahead of it.
2. Make sure that your happy place is free from diversions and interruptions so that you can achieve deep thought.
3. It's okay to try different locations over several retreats. It is about finding the perfect spot for you that will allow you to maximize the benefits of your personal retreat.
4. Consider taking a class and learning a new skill, craft, or art.

Worksheet:
Where to take your Personal Retreat

Part 1: Assessing Your Ideal Retreat Location

1. What type of environment do you find most conducive to relaxation, reflection, and creativity?

_____

_____

_____

2. Are you drawn to natural settings like the mountains or the beach, or would you prefer a more rural lake area or a desert location?

_____

_____

3. What kind of accommodation would best suit your needs and budget, such as a hotel room, cabin, or boarding house?

_____

_____

Part 2: Identifying Possible Retreat Locations

1. Research potential retreat locations based on your ideal environment and accommodation preferences.

_____

_____

_____

_____

_____

_____

_____

_____

_____

_____

2. Consider factors such as distance, travel time, and accessibility.

_____

_____

_____

_____

_____

3. Read reviews and gather information on the location's amenities and services to ensure they align with your needs and goals.

_____

_____

_____

_____

_____

Part 3: Comparing Retreat Locations

1. Create a list of potential retreat locations and compare them based on your ideal environment, accommodation preferences, and budget.

_____

_____

_____

_____

_____

_____

_____

_____

_____

_____

_____

_____

_____

_____

2. Consider factors such as the location's reputation, the availability of accommodations that align with your goals, and any additional costs or fees.

_____

_____

_____

_____

_____

_____

_____

_____

_____

_____

_____

_____

_____

_____

3. Rank each location based on how well it meets your needs and preferences.

_____

_____

_____

_____

_____

_____

_____

_____

_____

_____

_____

_____

_____

_____

_____

_____

Part 4: Choosing Your Retreat Location

1. Evaluate your list of potential retreat locations and choose the one that best meets your needs and goals.

_____

_____

_____

_____

_____

_____

_____

_____

_____

2. If necessary, confirm availability and make reservations.

_____

_____

3. If you have any concerns or questions, contact the location directly to address them.

_____

Part 5: Preparing for Your Retreat

1. Research the area surrounding your retreat location, including nearby restaurants, grocery stores, and other services.

_____

_____

_____

_____

_____

_____

_____

_____

_____

_____

_____

_____

_____

_____

2. Make a packing list based on the location's climate, amenities, and activities.

_____

_____

_____

_____

_____

_____

_____

_____

_____

_____

_____

_____

3. Consider any special preparations you may need to make, such as arranging pet care or notifying your employer or family of your absence.

_____

_____

_____

_____

Part 6: Reflection

1. After your retreat, reflect on the location you chose. Did it meet your needs and expectations?

   _____

   _____

   _____

2. Consider whether you would choose the same location again or prefer to try a different location for your next retreat.

   _____

— ◯ —

Remember, choosing the right retreat location is key to a successful personal retreat. Use this worksheet to help you assess your ideal environment, identify potential locations, and select the one that best meets your needs and goals.

— Step 3 —

SETTING REALISTIC GOALS AND ACHIEVING THEM

Deciding on and setting achievable goals during your personal retreat boils down to understanding what goals are and how you can reach them. When I say goal, I simply mean an intention or objective that you want to attain. Goals are not "wishes." Merely stating, "I wish I had a million dollars," or "I wish I had the boss's job" are not goals. Wishes lack the substance of follow-through. While it is effortless to harbor wishes, the path to realizing one's intentions demands sacrifices. You need to be honest with yourself regarding your willingness to go the extra mile and relinquish immediate gratification and comfort, with the understanding that these sacrifices will ultimately yield the desired outcomes and greater rewards. The setting and evaluation of goals is a core principle of your personal retreat.

Do you have the ability and the stamina to make those kinds of sacrifices? To sacrifice whatever you need to in order to reach your goals? If not, it is pointless to continue reading this information because you may not be ready to take full advantage of going on a personal retreat. But, if you have what it takes, achieving your desires is within reach once you lay out your plan and sit with it in deep thought on your personal retreat.

I am talking about realistic goals here, not pie-in-the-sky

goals that are unobtainable, like one day living on Mars—that will likely not happen in our lifetime. No, I am talking about goals you have a good chance of reaching if you work your butt off to attain them.

The SMART method is a popular goal-setting framework used in personal and professional settings. SMART stands for Specific, Measurable, Achievable, Relevant, and Time-bound.[27] This is an excellent guide to use when setting goals while on your personal retreat.

Specific goals are clear and well-defined, with a defined outcome. Suppose someone is working on their fitness. A general goal might be "I want to get in shape," but a specific goal using SMART would be "I want to lose ten pounds in the next three months by following a daily workout routine and eating a balanced diet."

Measurable goals can be tracked and quantified, providing a sense of progress and achievement. For instance, if you have a goal to enhance your productivity at work, a measurable goal would be, "I aim to increase my weekly sales calls from 50 to 75 over the next two months."

Achievable goals are realistic and attainable, taking into account your skills, resources, and limitations. If you're an entry-level employee aspiring to become a CEO in a year, your goal might not be achievable. Instead, an achievable goal would be, "I plan to earn a promotion to a mid-level manager within the next two years by gaining additional qualifications and consistently delivering exceptional performance."

Relevant goals align with your values, aspirations, and priorities, ensuring they are meaningful and motivating. If someone's passion lies in environmental conservation, a relevant goal might be, "I want to reduce my household's carbon footprint by 30 percent in the next year by adopting eco-friendly practices and making sustainable choices in my daily life."

Finally, time-bound goals are linked to a specific timeframe or deadline, helping to maintain focus and accountability. A time-bound goal for someone aspiring to write a book could be "I intend to finish writing my three-hundred-page novel within the next 12 months by dedicating at least two hours every day to writing."

By applying the SMART method during your personal retreat, you can formulate clear and effective goals that are specific, measurable, achievable, relevant, and time-bound, ultimately guiding you toward personal and professional growth, which is one of your retreat's purposes.

We make plans to do something, and then we don't take the action necessary to follow through on those plans. That is called procrastination. We have all experienced it, and some even live in a perpetual state of procrastination. There is a very good reason for this: we like instant gratification, which means we have an aversion to long-term payoff. In other words, we are conditioned to value getting something immediately—satisfy the present, the now—over the future benefits of delaying that want. Yet, by having the ability to delay that pleasure until some point in the future when we reach our goal, there is a greater chance we will be successful. Being able to resist that urge now will allow you to close the divide between where you currently are and where you want to be. Being conscious of the allure of instant gratification will help you think rationally about reaching your goals. Those who can master this will see it pay dividends in how quickly you can achieve your goals.

Poet and novelist Victor Hugo suffered from procrastination. He once promised a new book to his publisher on a specific timeline. Instead of writing on a schedule, Hugo spent his time doing everything other than writing. Frustrated by the author, his publisher finally set a six-month deadline for him to deliver the book. Trying to break his procrastination habit, Hugo gathered up all his clothing and had his assistant take them away, leaving himself with only a shawl to cover his body.[28] Hugo, unable to go outdoors, remained in his study writing until he completed the novel, *The Hunchback of Notre Dame*, which was ultimately released two weeks ahead of schedule[29]. This may be an extreme case for battling procrastination, but it worked for Hugo. He forced himself to stick to the writing schedule and deadline imposed by his publisher because he had no clothes to do anything else.

Hugo had a goal to finish his novel in six months, and he took the necessary action to meet that future goal. As an unusual approach, he had his clothing locked away by his assistant. This left him no choice but to start writing. In effect, Hugo reduced the obstacles or *friction* that he was experiencing in getting started on the novel by getting rid of the one thing that would prevent him from leaving his home. That allowed Hugo to break his procrastination habit and reach his goal.

The procrastination habit can be beaten if you can recognize that it is preventing you from reaching your goal. Often, it is not the work itself that is hard, but the starting of the work. If you can break through that, you will be on your way to completing whatever work is needed to reach your goal. That is and should be a goal that you can deal with on your personal retreat. Analyze why you might procrastinate, and then, using the SMART method, make it a goal not to procrastinate anymore.

Most of us have more than one goal, which is an excellent thing. Having more than one goal is vitally important so that you always strive to reach something and stay engaged. You never want to reach a goal and then say, "Well, I'm done—there is nothing else for me to look forward to." If you do that, then you will have given up on living. That is why you have to write down all your goals and then prioritize them in a logical order. Doing so will allow you to tackle one goal at a time instead of spreading yourself too thin by working on many goals simultaneously. Working toward too many goals at once can leave you frustrated and more likely to give up. Your personal retreat will help you organize your goals in a logical order. Once in the rhythm of taking a personal retreat, you will be able to review the past year's goals and set new goals for the coming year.

Think of yourself in a small open sailboat. The sails are up to catch the wind, and you have a rudder on the transom of the boat to guide you toward your destination—your goal. If you have multiple goals and continue to tack back and forth from one goal to the next, you will find yourself doing a lot of work and not reaching any one goal, only zigzagging around in circles. If you sail toward one goal at a time, you will have set a course to get from where you are to your priority goal before charting a course to the next goal. You use your energy efficiently to reach each goal in a specified order.

My goal as a writer was to write this book to share what I know about taking a personal retreat and expanding my creativity that I have developed over decades. To do that, I had a writing schedule each day that set out how many words a day I needed to write to complete this book by a certain date. If I stuck to my plan, the schedule, I'd hit my milestones and complete this book by that specified date, the deadline. I could have procrastinated doing any number of things, but I didn't because I set my goal to write each day.

It really is that easy, and once you realize that you can take any goal and break it down into smaller, more achievable milestones, you'll see how quickly you can reach some of your own goals. I was able to write the first draft of this book in less than 60 days.

Suppose your goal is to run your first marathon. You will create a schedule of running a certain distance every day or every other day, increasing your distance each week to condition your body until you reach the required length to finish the marathon. The goal is to complete your first marathon, and the schedule or plan is the process by which you will achieve that goal. Without the plan, then you are a rudderless boat. The intention points you in a direction, and the plan determines your progress in reaching that goal. This is why setting goals is so important to each of us in order to get the most out of the life we want.

How does an Olympic athlete win a gold medal? The athlete will spend years training and conditioning their body to become the best at their chosen sport or activity. They will work with coaches and trainers following a specific regimen and schedule of workouts. The athlete will participate in competitions with other athletes that qualify them to possibly compete in the Olympics. They are continuously working out, training, and competing with one goal in mind: to be the best. For the athlete who is serious about their intention, it is all consuming until they reach their goal.[30]

Once they have achieved that goal, they will set their sights on new goals, winning more gold and possibly participating in more than one Olympics. Michael Phelps won 28 medals, 23 of them gold, competing in five Olympics, and was the oldest individual gold medalist in swimming history before retiring. He was quoted during his training years as saying, "Eat, sleep and swim. That's all I can do...it became a job." Phelps dedicated himself to achieving his goal and, in the process, set many records while becoming the best swimmer in the world. [31]

Michael Phelps is a prime example of the focus and dedication you must have to achieve your goals. I'm not saying that you will reach the lofty heights of the Olympics, but it is a great example of drive and determination. The important lesson here is that you must focus on your goal. This is one of the reasons that taking a personal retreat to your happy place is critical in helping you identify your true goals in life. It may require that you take an assessment of your priorities and put some of the less important things aside for now or jettison them for good. Streamlining your priorities and concentrating on one intention at a time will result in real progress toward reaching that goal. Once reached, you can then start to build off that accomplishment to reach the next goal and so on. It requires focus, effort, and determination.

But just saying it won't make it happen. Writing down your goal and the plan to achieve it has been proven in scientific studies to be more effective than just verbally committing to it.[32] Try this simple exercise: write in your journal or set an appointment on your calendar to take a vigorous 30-minute walk three times this week or next, say Monday, Wednesday, and Friday. Write down the day, dates, and times you will take your walk. You'll be surprised to see that because you have written it down and looked at it several times, you'll be more likely to follow through on that intention.

This is called *implementation intentions* by psychologists, "an implementation intention supports this goal intention by setting out in advance when, where and how I will achieve this goal."[33] What you are doing with the implementation behavior is making a pre-decision to go for that vigorous walk, which does not require you to make another decision because you have made it already, written it down, and will review it several times before doing it just through the mere fact that you look at your calendar regularly. You are embedding in your subconscious the idea that you will be going for those walks on certain days, at certain times, and you'll go because you have reduced the friction, the resistance of procrastination, in the decision-making process. I do this as a routine with my weekly exercise schedule and other tasks that are prone to procrastination.

On Sunday mornings, I make a series of entries on my computer calendar indicating the days and times I will be doing my workouts for the upcoming week. Once those color-coded entries are on my calendar, I look at them intentionally, both consciously and subconsciously, on a continual basis as I schedule other appointments, conference calls, and engagements on my calendar in the coming days and weeks. This has directly impacted me doing those workouts when I intended to and not procrastinating or pushing them off to another day. These weekly workouts have become a habit over time, which has turned into a regular routine that has gone on autopilot—meaning, I no longer think consciously about doing the workout; I just do it. It works for my exercise routine and other intentions that may be challenging to start and complete.

Having a specific plan for your intention or goal, indicating where, when, and what you are going to do, will increase your chances of success, especially if you focus on one thing at a time. As I mentioned and want to keep emphasizing, when you set out to achieve a big goal, break it down into a series of mini-goals that allow you to focus on accomplishing each mini-goal on the path to realizing the big goal. Doing this makes you focus your energy and consciousness on one goal at a time until that step becomes automatic. Studies have shown that for a habit to fully form and "stick," it will likely take a few months.[34] That said, it depends on the complexity and level of difficulty of the new habit, your genetic makeup, your environment, and the level of focus and commitment you give to achieving your goals.[35] The clear fact is that if you are honest with yourself and diligently work to achieve your goals, you will reach them in time. You must believe in yourself and your ability to reach the results you desire and commit to the hard work required. If you can do this successfully, even through setbacks and failures, you will eventually achieve the results you want.

There is no magic elixir, no genie who will grant you a wish. It is just you and your unfettered desire to reach your goals. At some point, you will have to look yourself in the mirror, be truthful, and decide what goal you want to reach or what new path you want to take with your life. It is *your* decision, not anyone else's. No one else will do it for you, and if you think they will, you'll be waiting a very long time for something that may never materialize. It is up to you to take control of your life and make your dreams a reality.

Again, progress toward your goals does come more quickly

when you focus on one goal at a time. When you have multiple goals, you split your focus and do not give any single goal the attention it needs. By simply prioritizing your goals and focusing your energy on one at a time, you will see more progress than if you continued to service several different goals all at once. This is even more true when you break down each goal into its individual components.

I mentioned earlier that on one of my personal retreats to my happy place, I wrote out a list of books I wanted to write. That list had eight book titles on it. These were book titles that I was passionate about and thought I could write because I knew the subject matter intimately. The old saying, "Write what you know," resonated with me, and I felt I could tackle these subjects effectively. The list focused on topics and projects that I was part of and wanted to document in writing. I was enthusiastic and pumped about these subjects, but I only focused on writing one book at a time. If I had tried to work on each title simultaneously, I would not have completed any one book. I would have been jumping back and forth between them all with a diffuse focus and not have finished one that would have been good enough to be published. I wrote one book, then turned in that manuscript and started on the next. I repeated that process over and over.

As each book was completed, I crossed it off the list. I added more topics and titles to the list that I wanted to cover during subsequent retreats. Each year, when I head up to my happy place in Maine, one of my intentions is to review my book-writing list. I will spend several hours or even half a day just looking at my list, crossing off a title or two I've completed, and adding new topics. My writing list is fluid and continuously changing from year to year, but what is consistent is that I review and modify it on a regular basis. That represents one goal for me: to continue writing and publishing books.

That is not to say you can't do some minor tasks associated with other goals. Although I focused my attention on writing one book at a time, I did devote some time to gathering research for other future projects. It is a natural process because of how my day is scheduled. I write in the mornings and read in the afternoons, among other things. I may be reading the newspaper and come across an article that is relevant to a future project, and I will add it to the research folder for that book project. Often, I have come across a new book release that is of interest, and I may order it as part of the research for some other project I have on the back burner. I will read other books that touch on a topic or have some reference to another project and will make notes or highlight passages I may wish to reference when I begin work on that topic. Some may view all this as multitasking, but it is not.

Multitasking is just doing multiple tasks at the same time. Some people consider it a badge of honor to be able to do many things at once. To me, it brings to mind the old adage, "Jack of all trades, master of none." Maybe you know someone like this. They seem to be constantly doing multiple things but never really accomplish anything to a level of quality and completion, considering their efforts.

We have all experienced watching television and doing some other tasks, whether reading, knitting, or paying the bills. That is a form of multitasking and is certainly the definition of doing more than one thing at a time. You are likely focused only on the one thing, say paying the bills, while the television is on in the background. You may take a moment and look up at the game that is on to see a play or the score, which is shifting focus from one task, paying the bills, to the other, watching television. It is nearly impossible to do more than one meaningful task at the same time when it requires serious concentration and focus.

Doing a complex task requires that your brain focus only on one job at a time. Switching back and forth between different tasks costs you more time because your brain must take additional time to re-focus each time you switch. Researchers at Loughborough University in London did a study[36] of workers at a firm and their reaction times to being interrupted while working to check their emails. They found that the workers, on average, checked their emails about every five minutes. It was also noted that each interruption required more than a minute of recovery time to get back to the same work level they were at prior to the email interruption.

One can conclude from this example that multitasking has a negative time cost— the more multitasking you engage in, the more time you will waste. By staying focused on one task at a time, especially during your retreat, you will work more efficiently and achieve your goals more quickly, allowing you to move on to the next task. In other words, as mentioned earlier, breaking down a goal into a series of mini-goals and accomplishing each mini-goal on its own before moving to the next will help you reach the main goal faster. So, doing one thing at a time as best as you can will ultimately be more time-efficient in driving toward your larger end goal.

I will generally pick one major task to accomplish each day, along with other things I need to get done throughout a typical workday. I write every day, so my main goal each day is to write at least one thousand words, if I can, on the one project I am currently working on. Now, I may not reach that goal of one thousand words a day because some days it comes in under, and other days it will go over that amount. I am okay with that because, on average, it does work out to be more than one thousand words a day. That sounds like a lot, but in reality, it boils down to about four to five typed, double-spaced pages. To me, that is a doable goal that I have stuck to for quite some time. Ernest Hemingway wrote five hundred words a day. Stephen King writes two thousand words a day that yields 180,000 in three months, which he believes is the "maximum amount of time it should take someone to finish a first draft."[37] We all have to work at a pace that is comfortable for us. Each of us has to set our own bar as to how much we wish to accomplish each day.

I am an advocate of setting big goals. That may be daunting at first, but as I have said, when you break these bold goals down into smaller goals, it becomes more manageable. For it to succeed, you have to set those smaller goals realistically so that if you work at them, you will reach them daily/weekly. It will be demoralizing to set lofty, unattainable goals for each day or week that you cannot possibly attain. If you do that, you will abandon your larger goals before you ever scratch the surface of reaching them. That is why it is important to write down the tasks needed to be accomplished in each step to reach the larger goal. Doing this in meaningful and doable chunks or mini-goals will make you feel good about each step as it is completed. As each step is completed, cross it off your list, which is a very gratifying thing to do.

What I have learned from more than 30 years of taking personal retreats to my happy place is that you have to find your own happy *zone* between sustainability and burnout.

Sustainability is all about maintaining a work ethic at a pace toward your individual goals at a rate you can preserve over a long period of time. If you work toward your goals at too high a rate that is impossible to sustain, you will experience burnout. You will be exhausted in a very short period of time.

In essence, burnout is the physical and mental collapse of your efforts to achieve some kind of goal. You give up because you don't have the stamina to continue pushing forward. You must avoid striving at such a high level that you burn yourself out and give up on trying to reach your overall goal. Taking a retreat will give you the time to think through a thorough plan for reaching your goals without risking burnout or giving up.

Often, people get supercharged about reaching a lofty goal they have set and go headlong into doing everything possible to reach that goal quickly. They work at an unrelenting, unsustainable pace and get so exhausted they give up because they just physically cannot go any further. That is the last thing you want to do when you set a goal. You must have a sense of purpose in how you will achieve your goal, and that starts with setting some limits on yourself. Think of it as not exceeding your own personal speed limit.

You must understand why the goal you have set is important and how you are going to track your performance. What does the goal mean to you? If you are unsure or don't know why it is important, then it is just some random thing, and you need to rethink it. If you fully grasp why the goal is important, you will also understand how breaking it down into manageable chunks will help you complete the larger goal. By completing each chunk or mini-goal, you will be able to easily track your progress toward reaching the larger goal.

One of the best pieces of advice I ever read was from Steven King's book *On Writing: A Memoir of Craft.* He said, "Amateurs sit and wait for inspiration, the rest of us just get up and go to work."[38] For me, that means I sit at my desk every day and write toward my goal of one thousand words. By writing each day, I am working toward my larger goal of completing a particular book, article, or writing assignment. By not writing, I am idle and not moving forward toward reaching that goal. It's not about waiting to be struck by the lightning of a great idea; it's not about having the right pen or journal; it's not about the planets aligning perfectly and knowing the result will surely be successful. None of that matters. It is all about doing. You must be dedicated to working at your goals, whatever they are, each day in a measured and meaningful way.

Sitting around making excuses about why you have not started working toward your goals will only delay getting started. Wishing for something will not do it; you have to roll up your shirtsleeves and begin working toward achieving each goal. The best way is to show up every day and work at it. Whatever your goal is, you must take the necessary steps to build the momentum to reach it. Surrounding yourself with the optimal environment will help that process. You have to start somewhere. Every journey we take starts with the first step.

It all starts with the system you put in place around you to strive for consistent progress toward your goal. Creating a space where you can spend whatever amount of time you need to examine, study, and plan to work toward your goal is important. Whether doing research, writing emails, reading, or creating, you need an environment conducive to doing that work. A place free of distractions will help you focus on formulating your goals. You can give a lot of thought to finding that space while on a personal retreat. That space may be a closet that you can sit down in the middle of to write, a bathroom where you can have peace of mind, or a private office that is your sanctuary. But it is important to figure out where your space is during the year, between your annual personal retreat.

I have found it best to have a place where you can just be alone for a period of time, even if that is going to the local library and reserving a small private study room or just sitting in a quiet corner. You can even go to a local park and sit on a bench or lay out a blanket on a lawn away from any activity that may be going on.

Regardless of your situation, you can always find a quiet spot someplace if you are serious about formulating and working toward your goals. Just remember there are no excuses; there are only solutions, no matter what situation you find yourself in. There are plenty of stories of people who had nothing and have achieved incredible success by staying focused and going after their goals. The key for them was to have solid goals, a plan to work hard at reaching them, and, most importantly, never giving up. You must, first and foremost, believe in yourself because no one else will until you do.

Quick Tips:

1. Deciding on and setting achievable goals boils down to understanding what goals are and how they are reached.

2. Wishes are nothing more than goals not followed through on.

3. Progress toward your goals comes more quickly when you focus on one goal at a time.

4. Having a specific plan for your intention or goal, indicating where, when, and what you are going to do, will increase your chances of success.

5. Psychologists define implementation intentions as setting out in advance the when, where, and how you will achieve your goal. By writing it down, you have already made the decision to do it.

6. Sitting around making excuses about why you have not started working toward your goals will only delay getting started.

<u>*Worksheet:*</u>
Setting Realistic Goals and Achieving Them on a Personal Retreat

Part 1: Assessing Your Current Goals

1. What are your current goals, both personal and professional?

_____

_____

_____

_____

_____

_____

_____

_____

_____

2. How realistic and achievable are your current goals?

_____

_____

3. Are your current goals aligned with your values and priorities?

_____

Part 2: Setting New Goals

1. What new goals do you want to set for yourself during your personal retreat?

_____

_____

_____

_____

_____

2. How will these new goals help you achieve your long-term vision for your life?

_____

_____

_____

_____

_____

3. How can you make these new goals realistic and achievable?

_____

_____

_____

_____

_____

Part 3: Defining Your Goals

1. Define each goal using the SMART method: specific, measurable, achievable, relevant, and time-bound.

_____

_____

_____

_____

_____

_____

_____

_____

_____

_____

_____

2. Break each goal down into smaller, actionable steps.

_____

_____

_____

_____

_____

_____

_____

_____

_____

_____

_____

_____

3. Determine any potential challenges or obstacles to achieving each goal.

_____

_____

_____

_____

_____

Part 4: Creating an Action Plan

1. Create an action plan for achieving each goal, including a timeline for completing each step.

_____

_____

_____

_____

_____

_____

_____

_____

_____

2. Identify any resources or support you may need to achieve each goal.

_____

_____

_____

_____

3. Consider any potential setbacks or roadblocks and develop strategies for overcoming them.

_____

_____

_____

_____

_____

Part 5: Implementing Your Action Plan

1. Begin implementing your action plan, starting with the first step.

_____

_____

_____

_____

2. Track your progress toward each goal and adjust your action plan as needed.

_____

_____

_____

_____

3. Celebrate your achievements along the way to stay motivated and inspired.

_____

_____

Part 6: Reflection

1. After your personal retreat, reflect on the goals you set and the progress you made toward achieving them.

_____

_____

_____

_____

_____

_____

2. Consider any insights or lessons you gained during your retreat that can help you continue to work toward your goals.

    _____

    _____

    _____

    _____

    _____

    _____

    _____

3. Create a plan for maintaining momentum and continuing to work toward your goals in your daily life.

    _____

    _____

    _____

    _____

    _____

    _____

    _____

Remember, setting and achieving realistic goals is key to personal growth and development. Use this worksheet to help you assess your current goals, set new goals, define each goal using the SMART method, create an action plan, and implement your plan during your personal retreat.

— *Step 4* —

JOURNALING YOUR INTENTIONS AND GOALS

Once you have determined the duration, timing, and location of your retreat, the next step is to identify the purpose and intentions that will guide your solitary sojourn. What thoughts and reflections will you immerse yourself in during this dedicated time? Perhaps unresolved relationship matters or career decisions have been lingering in your mind. Yet, you haven't had the opportunity to thoroughly contemplate them, resulting in a sense of stagnation. It is possible you are avoiding some issues in your life that genuinely warrant your attention and thoughtful consideration. Many individuals tend to avoid or procrastinate about those matters, knowing deep down that they require immediate attention but continuously deferring them for a later time. Unfortunately, that "later time" seldom arrives due to persistent avoidance. To ensure that you confront and address any pertinent issues, establish clear intentions for your retreat prior to embarking on it. This proactive approach will enable you to direct your focus toward the areas that demand resolution and provide a conducive environment for introspection and growth.

Intentions and goals, while related, serve different purposes. Intentions are the guiding principles or values that steer our actions and decisions. They set the moral compass for our lives. Goals, on the other hand, are the specific, measurable targets we aim to achieve in alignment with our intentions. Let me illustrate this with an example from the world of animation. In creating Disney's classic film *The Lion King*, one of the core intentions was to convey the importance of family and the circle of life. In this case, a corresponding goal might be to "craft a compelling and emotionally resonant scene where Simba, the protagonist, reunites with his long-lost father, Mufasa, under the stars." The intention guides the storytelling, while the goal defines a concrete outcome within the film that brings the intention to life.

While intentions and goals serve different purposes, your intentions are, at their essence, your goals. These may bubble up naturally once you start to let your mind wander. You may have given thought to them already. I usually have some sense of what I'd like to focus on when I take my retreats. Typically, I have a few goals I want to consider, which I have written down in my journal, and a topic or two that I want to spend time thinking about. These are two different things. One is the goals I set for myself: finish writing this book, lose some weight, exercise more, and plan to accomplish those goals. The others are more global topics like where I want to be in five or ten years in my career or if I could live anywhere, where I would move to. These are often larger, life-changing goals that require deep thinking. Often, the overarching topics will spawn smaller goals that can put you on the track to make these larger life decisions.

I see this as finding a balance between knowing the goals I

want to set and the ideas that naturally rise to the surface when I let my mind go or daydream. For your first few retreats, it may be helpful to write down a list of topics you want to dwell on, such as your job, family, long-term career, aspirations, dreams, and those "someday I will" desires. The physical act of writing down your intentions will make them more real—as will coming up with a loose schedule for your retreat.

This does not mean laying out a spreadsheet or a tight schedule that has every hour mapped out so that at 10:00 AM, I will think about my spouse; at 11:00 AM, give some thought to my job, and so on. No, it doesn't work that way. I know plenty of accountants, engineers, and other professionals think on the left side of their brains and feel this is the only way to plan any event, meeting, or retreat. But that is not what this solo retreat warrants. You have to look at Find Your Happy Place as more of a creative endeavor where you will spend as much time as possible on the right side—more creative side—of your brain.

What I'm talking about is a looser arrangement of thinking that requires getting away from the rigidity of your normal work life. You must view this process more creatively, allowing your mind to explore and think of whatever comes across your consciousness.

Believe it or not, this may be hard for some to do at the beginning as they are used to working strictly on the logical, analytical left side of their brain. There are a variety of exercises you can do to help you work on the right side of the brain. One is to learn something new, whether from a book or a class, as I have discussed previously and have done over the decades of taking my retreats. Taking a class in the creative arts will get your creativity flowing and have you thinking differently about things. You could also doodle or just write about anything in longhand.

I have found the classic book Drawing on the Right Side of the Brain by Betty Edwards[39] superior in its instruction for tapping into the creative side of your abilities. It offers a series of simple exercises you can do anywhere that will help you develop your creativity further. The book is especially relevant for anyone who works on the left side of their brain most of the time.

Back to your list of intentions. I think the best way to start creating a list of intentions for your retreat is to contemplate what you need clarity on now. This could be anything from where your career is heading to making a major life change, like moving or ditching your career for another, to how you would like to improve or rejuvenate a relationship.

Sometimes, a relationship stagnates. It becomes so routine and familiar that you become bored or feel stuck. Add it to your list. You already know what all these things are because they cross your mind daily while you are sitting in traffic, staring out the window at work, or riding the elevator to an appointment. These are things that pop into our minds, and we often push them aside because we don't want to deal with them at that moment. It is either painful or frustrating, and you "kick that can down the road." Those are exactly the issues you want to add to your list of intentions for your solo retreat.

Don't worry about how you are going to fix this or change that now; just write down the topics that have been weighing on your mind over the past year or longer. Typically, I will have three to five things I want to give deep thought to, but there is no exact number. One year, I sat for a week thinking about only one thing—a career change. Try to keep the number of topics realistic so you can give the greatest amount of attention to each while on your retreat. I recommend you not exceed five items on your list of what's most pressing and important to you. It is better to keep the number of items less than more so that you can put quality time into each. Having just one item is perfectly fine as well. There is nothing wrong with thinking exclusively about your relationships, career, or any other topic. The retreat should be as productive as possible without being overwhelming. It should be leisurely and relaxing while you are thinking and planning.

Every year, when I go to my happy place in Maine, with no more than five things on my list of intentions, I am not concerned about what order they are in or when I will spend time thinking about each. That doesn't matter at all. What matters most is that I have a handful of topics I want to sit with, and I have written them down.

When you draw up your own list, remember—nothing is trivial if it's important to you. You could include something as simple as your intention to relax and enjoy the natural environment around you or as deep as how to change your career path and leave your current job for a more fulfilling and rewarding one. Both are valid and will take the amount of time each requires, no more or no less.

I recommend you get a journal and write your list down on the first page. This doesn't have to be some fancy leather-bound diary with a lock and key. In fact, please don't waste money on such a thing—a very simple college-ruled composition notebook works great. I buy these a half-dozen at a time online, and they cost me a dollar or a dollar and a half each. I even picked one up at a discount store for fifty cents once. They are perfect for daily journaling, and it's okay to scribble out mistakes or leave in misspellings. You can draw diagrams, pictures, or doodles. You can be neat or sloppy; it doesn't matter because only you will read and refer back to it. All that matters is that you can understand what you have written or drawn.

I usually fill up about three or four college-ruled composition notebooks a year. I write on both sides of the page. When I am on my retreat, I will journal every morning longhand at least two or three pages to get my creative juices flowing. To me, journaling is a way to loosen up my thinking, and the physical act of writing helps stimulate the creative process. Writing longhand slows everything down and allows for ideas to wholly form and emerge. It lets your thoughts fully engage and connect in a way they don't when you're typing quickly on a keyboard. By writing longhand, you are allowing your ideas to shift, morph, and change by the sheer nature of slowing down and writing it all out by hand.

When you are writing by hand, you are giving yourself the necessary time to think through your thoughts before you write them down. You can take your time to choose the right words or phrasing and where to break for a new paragraph or not. Those words and phrases will have more emotional impact because you took the time to think about the choice. That, in turn, will contribute to the feeling you want to convey in the passage. Longhand gives you the opportunity to ponder your writing. By slowing down your writing, you develop a deeper, more meaningful connection to whatever story or experience you're writing about. For me, the blank page is a canvas I paint with words using the writing implement of my choice.

Longhand taps into the creative side of your brain to bring out imaginative solutions to the issues and topics you are thinking and writing about. It has been proven that the physical act of writing longhand increases neural activity in certain sections of the brain.[40] Researchers, using advanced imaging tools, have found "that writing by hand is more than just a way to communicate. The practice helps with learning letters and shapes, can improve idea composition and expression, and may aid fine motor-skill development."[41] In other words, writing longhand makes you pay more attention and think more deeply about your writing, increasing your creativity and problem-solving abilities.

Another aspect of writing longhand is the convenience of

being able to sit anywhere with a pen and notebook. I once spent an afternoon sitting at an old wooden picnic table on the edge of a cove, writing part of this book longhand. I could look up periodically and stare out at the sunlight sparkling on the water and the distant pine-covered islands. I was thinking about what I would write next, deciding my word choice and how I wanted to construct my thoughts on paper. There were no distractions with the clickety-clacking sounds of my fingers tapping on the keyboard. No internet, email, or social media to break my thought process. I didn't have to worry about the battery draining on the computer or whether there were electrical outlets where I was going to sit— it didn't matter. It all aids in the deep immersion into your thoughts and purposeful storytelling on paper as you write by hand.

Writing longhand is a process that is not conducive to continuous editing, which is so easy to do as you type away on your computer in a Word document. There is no spellcheck, thesaurus, or formatting options. You are forced to be more definite with every word you write. If not, you will be scratching words and sentences out continuously. Slowing down and letting the words flow from your brain to your hand and then onto the paper involves your senses— visualizing what you want to write, seeing the words forming in your mind, hearing the pen rolling across the page, and feeling the grip of the writing implement on the paper. It is a tactile delight to the senses.

There is a meditative quality to being able to slow down and handwrite words on paper using a pen or pencil. Writing by hand is deliberate and thoughtful, with a cadence, a beat, and a rhythm. Your hand gliding back and forth across the page helps to enhance deep thought, the depth of connection to your writing. The story you are telling can be written down in a slower, more consequential manner; it will be more meaningful since writing longhand naturally allows you to dig further into the emotional truth of your own writing and storytelling.

Aside from stimulating the creative side of your brain, writing longhand may also be the easiest cognitive exercise for keeping your mind sharp as you age. Researchers have seen dramatic changes in patients who brought in journals from age 55 to 70. P. Murali Doraiswamy, a neuroscientist at Duke University, said, "As more people lose writing skills and migrate to the computer, retraining people in handwriting skills could be a useful cognitive exercise."[42] There are benefits to writing by hand every day, even just jotting down a description of something you saw while you were out and about during your day that was memorable or struck your imagination. Writing down notes, observations, and descriptions will pay dividends in keeping your mind sharp.

The benefits are overwhelming when it comes to journaling, not just on your personal retreat but daily. I generally start my day journaling, and as I fill a notebook, I start a new one. Those composition notebooks are part diary, part catharsis, part therapy, and part idea log. It is a place where you can jot down your hopes, desires, fears, goals, and anything else that comes to mind for your eyes only. You can dump whatever you are feeling into the notebook, knowing it is yours alone. You can keep your notebooks or periodically purge them if you want. I keep mine and have referred back to them years later, recalling an idea I wrote or a story I now have distance from and want to write about more fully. Journaling is just a healthy, creative habit, and there is no better time to start journaling than when you begin planning your personal retreat.

Quick Tips:

1. If you don't already do it, then start journaling as soon as you are in the planning stages of your personal retreat.
2. Begin by writing down your intentions for the retreat and the goals that you wish to achieve.
3. Writing longhand in your journal has a cognitive effect and will pay dividends in keeping your mind sharp.
4. Longhand taps into the creative side of your brain to bring out imaginative solutions to the issues and topics you are thinking and writing about.

Worksheet:
Journaling Your Intentions and Goals on a Personal Retreat

Part 1: Assessing Your Current Goals

1. What is your primary intention for this personal retreat?

_____

_____

_____

_____

2. What specific outcomes or results do you hope to achieve during your retreat?

_____

_____

_____

_____

2. What personal, professional, or spiritual issues do you want to explore or work on during your retreat?

_____

_____

_____

_____

_____

_____

Part 2: Defining Your Goals

1. What specific goals do you want to achieve during your personal retreat?

   _____

   _____

   _____

   _____

   _____

   _____

2. What steps will you need to take to achieve each goal?

   _____

   _____

   _____

   _____

   _____

   _____

   _____

3. How will you measure your progress toward each goal?

_____

_____

_____

Part 3: Journaling Your Intentions and Goals

1. Set aside time each day during your retreat to journal about your intentions and goals.

_____

_____

2. Begin each journal entry by restating your primary intention for the retreat and reviewing the specific goals you want to achieve.

_____

_____

3. Reflect on your progress toward each goal and any insights or lessons you have gained during your retreat.

_____

_____

Part 4: Tracking Your Progress

1. Create a tracker or "spreadsheet" to help you monitor your progress toward each goal.

   _____

   _____

2. Update your tracker daily with any progress or achievements toward each goal.

   _____

   _____

3. Reflect on your progress regularly and adjust your goals or action steps as needed.

   _____

   _____

Part 5: Reflection

1. After your retreat, review your journal entries and tracker.

   _____

   _____

2. Reflect on your progress toward each goal and the insights or lessons you gained during your retreat.

_____

_____

_____

_____

3. Consider how you can integrate what you learned and achieved during your retreat into your daily life.

_____

_____

_____

_____

Remember, journaling your intentions and goals can be a powerful tool for personal growth and development. Use this worksheet to help you set your intentions, define your goals, and track your progress toward achieving them during your personal retreat.

Sidebar—Planning What to Bring on Your Retreat

Once you've sorted out the logistics of your retreat—when, where, and how long—it's time to strategize your packing. While it might seem like a no-brainer, I believe it demands careful consideration to avoid overpacking and ensure a successful retreat.

It's a common traveler's pitfall to overpack, lugging around items that go unused. I've been there, unpacking and wondering why I brought certain things I never touched. It's a habit I've managed to kick over the years. Some people slip into "survival mode," bringing as much as possible, even for a week-long vacation. I've seen travelers at airports with multiple oversized suitcases, though carry-on luggage would suffice for most.

Your retreat's location sets the tone for your clothing and footwear choices. Checking a ten-day weather forecast is a smart move, though it's surprisingly overlooked by some. In summer, opt for lightweight clothing like shorts, T-shirts, and pullovers. Don't forget swimwear if you're near water, unless, like me, you're certain you won't be swimming. For a winter retreat, pack appropriately for the cold. Layering is key, but remember that winter clothing can be bulky and might require a checked suitcase for a flight.

Check if your accommodations offer laundry facilities. It can reduce your packing load significantly, and I've found it a refreshing change from the norm. Consider wearing items multiple times, especially when your days involve deep thought and relaxation. Skip evening gowns, suits, or fancy attire. Avoid "what if" scenarios that detract from your retreat's purpose. Concentrate on essentials and remember why you're on a personal retreat, not a vacation.

When it comes to footwear, a pair of sneakers or hiking boots is usually sufficient. Leave dress shoes and high heels behind. I typically bring hiking boots, deck shoes or sneakers, and flip-flops, avoiding an excessive shoe collection.

If possible, opt for carry-on luggage. Efficient packing and carefully evaluating each item are crucial. However, for longer trips, checking a bag may be necessary. Practice mindful packing by leaving room for potential purchases and removing items from their packaging. Consider buying toiletries at your destination to avoid liquid restrictions when flying.

I've learned that rolling clothing is space-efficient and minimizes wrinkling. Utilize empty spaces in your luggage for items like socks and pack new purchases without their packaging.

Your personal retreat requires a "less is more" mindset. Focus on the essentials and minimize electronic gadgets to fully embrace introspection, reflection, and deep thought. While it's challenging to unplug entirely, strive to use your smartphone sparingly. Avoid the distractions of constant emails and social media. Keep your devices off during the day to maximize your retreat experience. This includes refraining from listening to music, which can divert your focus. Instead, immerse yourself in the natural sounds of your surroundings.

Efficient packing enhances your retreat by reducing wardrobe stress. You can wear the same items multiple times, making it less necessary to carry excess clothing. After over thirty years of personal retreats, I still review everything and pack as minimally as possible.

Consider multiple passes at packing, reevaluating your choices after a break. This iterative process improves with practice, like everything in a personal retreat. Remember, less is more!

— ᕤ —

Quick Tips:

1. The location of your retreat will dictate what you will need to bring for clothing and footwear.
2. Roll your clothing to maximize the space in your suitcase.
3. If you are flying to your retreat, consider purchasing toiletries, i.e., toothpaste, mouthwash, and shaving cream, at your destination.
4. Remember, less is more when packing for your personal retreat.

— Step 5 —

HEALTHY MIND, HEALTHY BODY

While we may not always be fully aware of it, maintaining a healthy mind and a vibrant imagination requires us to nurture a healthy body. This entails taking proper care of our physical well-being through exercise and nutrition. Consequently, one aspect of your retreat will naturally revolve around nourishing your body. This doesn't necessarily imply that you must embark on a strict diet or undergo a cleansing regimen. However, it also isn't the time to disregard caution and indulge in unhealthy junk food consumption. As you plan your retreat, it is crucial to consider what, where, and when you will have your meals. Depending on the location of your personal retreat, these meals can be purchased, prepared by yourself, or served to you. The planning process should include thoughtful deliberation regarding your nutritional choices, ensuring that your body receives the sustenance it needs to thrive during this period of reflection and rejuvenation.

I consider myself fortunate to have found a place where I can pay for room and board. The humble room accommodations I have on my annual retreat in Maine include three meals a day. Yes, I get three hots and a cot! This may not be the norm, but when planning your retreat, it is worth the effort to see if you can find accommodations that include daily meals or at least one or two meals. It might only be breakfast and dinner or just an evening meal, but it will be one less thing to think about. From my experience, you should be able to find plenty of bed and breakfast establishments all over the country, as well as boarding houses in the more remote or rural areas.

During my retreat, I have a choice every morning between a hot or cold breakfast or both if I want. For lunch, I can pick from three sandwiches and pick up my lunch at a central location mid-day. Each night at 6:00 PM, I have a hot dinner with plenty of choices. This isn't cafeteria food but rather good, hearty home cooking. There is always a vegetarian choice, and the kitchen is happy to accommodate any dietary requirements guests may have, from low sodium to gluten-free to nuts and other food allergies. I can also determine how big or small portions I want since the food is served family style—you serve yourself at breakfast and dinner. To me, family-style eating is a luxury when staying away from home.

Having the meal plan all in place means I don't have to think about it other than whether I want to eat at the boarding house. It gives me the ability to decide my day without any preset obligations. If I'm out for a drive or hike one afternoon and by dinner time I'm getting hungry, I can choose to stop at a roadside clam shack or a family-run restaurant serving lobster rolls. Once or twice during a weeklong retreat, I may go out to eat just for the change of scenery and pace. Having that flexibility is a treat. For me, it's important, for mind and body, to plan for my meals in advance.

As mentioned, you don't have to go on a diet, but the retreat is a good time to think about your nutritional habits. Have you been eating too much junk food, wolfing down a burger in your office as you stress over a deadline? Do you get home from work, throw a frozen dinner in the microwave, and eat in front of the television, washing the food down with a sugary beverage? Maybe it is time for you to look at your eating habits and think about making some changes. Doing so on your personal retreat is much easier than you think since you are alone and free from anyone else's influences. Changing your diet will likely make you feel and sleep better if you make good choices.

Being on your personal retreat will allow you to design a whole new meal plan for the days or week that you take for yourself. You don't have to, but it is a good way to become conscious of what you're consuming and whether you want to make a lifestyle adjustment. Your retreat is the perfect time to make changes to your food choices as it gives you time to develop a habit you can carry back to your normal everyday life. It is your choice.

You could decide to go vegetarian, which has health benefits like reducing the risk of high blood pressure and some types of cancer. It's not hard to do, even just for the time you are on your retreat. Depending on where you take your retreat, you may find places to eat that serve seasonal, local, wild, and organic foods. The farm-to-table movement, still popular, encourages restaurants to source their food locally. It is often refreshing because some restaurants change their menus daily based on what is available from their local suppliers. There is nothing like having a lobster or mussels pulled from the water that afternoon or experiencing the freshness of organic produce picked early in the day. Nothing is frozen; everything is fresh, and you can taste the difference, especially if your palette is used to a diet of frozen, processed, and packaged foods. More importantly, it will give you an opportunity to try new foods that may, in turn, help you change your regular diet for something healthier when you return home.

Another aspect of being on a retreat that you may want to consider is your intake of caffeine and other stimulants. Changing your routine gives you a great opportunity to either reduce or give up completely the amount of caffeine and other stimulants you ingest daily. Caffeine can boost your memory and mood and make you feel alert for at least a little while, but too much caffeine can also make you irritable.[43] Think about how many cups of coffee you had just today— maybe too many. I don't drink coffee; instead, I have a cup of black tea. It still gives me a little boost of caffeine but in a smaller dose than coffee. Reducing or eliminating these stimulants and toxins will aid in healing and strengthening your body.[44]

I was one of those people who drank Diet Coke morning, noon, and night. It was not uncommon for me to consume four or five sixteen-ounce bottles of diet soda a day. After reading reports on how the consumption of these beverages affects your health, I realized that I needed to stop drinking them. Many studies have shown that consuming diet soft drinks can cause serious health conditions, including diabetes, fatty liver, dementia, heart disease, and stroke.[45]

So, I set a goal to quit diet soda cold turkey on one of my retreats. When I arrived in Maine that year, I just stopped consuming diet soda and have not had another one since, and that was more than a decade ago. I feel much better for it and don't miss putting those chemicals in my body. Making that commitment was easy at the beginning of the two-week retreat because I was in a different environment with a different daily routine.

Along with changing your eating habits, you may want to use the time to adopt a new exercise routine during your retreat. There is an enormous body of research on the positive effects of regular physical activity on the body, brain, and cognition. The effects of aerobic physical activity on cognition and brain function at the molecular, cellular, systems and behavioral levels is an overwhelming factor that may lead to increased physical and mental health throughout life.[46] Exercise affects the brain in a number of ways, including pumping more oxygen to your gray matter. That, in turn, releases more hormones that increase brain cell growth, making it easier to grow new neuronal connections.[47] A study out of Stockholm, Sweden, correlated the "runner's high" with more cell growth in the hippocampus, an area of the brain responsible for learning and memory.[48]

This is one of the reasons that I incorporate some amount

of exercise into each day of my retreat. That doesn't mean I'm doing some strenuous aerobic workout or running ten miles uphill each day. What works for me is taking a walk or an easy hike. This can be between thirty minutes and an hour, depending on my motivation. I tend to do my walking in the mornings before I sit and begin my deep-thinking sessions. Walking increases my heart rate, pumping more oxygen to my brain. I am breathing in good, clean air, which makes me feel good all around. At home, I ride ten to twelve miles on a stationary bike in the mornings before sitting down to write. This daily activity feeds into the optimal use of my brain and my imagination and contributes to generally feeling upbeat due to the antidepressant effects of exercise.[49]

Exercise in relation to your personal retreat does not mean you have to sprint around a track or workout on a series of weight machines in the gym. No, the exercise I am advocating on a retreat is just being outside and going for a hike or long walk in nature. You don't need any special equipment or clothing, just a pair of sneakers or good hiking shoes.

The simple act of walking is proven to be good cardio exercise. Walking lowers your stress level and gives you more energy while building stamina. The act of walking briskly for a cardio workout strengthens your heart muscle and can lower your blood pressure and resting heart rate. Add to that the fact that regular cardio exercise from walking will sharpen your memory and mental focus.[50] All excellent reasons to plan on selecting a place that will allow you some walking time during your personal retreat.

Author, poet, and philosopher Henry David Thoreau wrote, "The benefit to me, to my life—I won't even say interior, I mean to the totality, in absolute terms—is immense: a long moment in which I look into myself, without being invaded by volatile, deafening hassles or alienated by the incessant cackle of characters. I capitalize myself with myself all day: a long moment in which I remain listening or in contemplation: and thus, nature lavishes all its colours [sic] on me." He went on to write, "On me alone. Walking magnifies receptiveness: I'm always receiving pure presence by the ton. All of that must obviously count for something. In the end, walking has been the more beneficial for being less profitable: what was given to me was given in profusion."[51]

Thoreau, author of the seminal work *Walden; or, Life in the Woods*, understood the true benefits of walking and walked four or five hours daily around Concord, Massachusetts, with his hands in his pockets thinking. "I think that I cannot preserve my health and spirits, unless I spend four hours a day at least—and it is commonly more than that—sauntering through the woods and over the hills and fields, absolutely free from all worldly engagements."[52] Walking allowed Thoreau to think deeply and formulate ideas and concepts that he then expanded upon in his many published works.

Frederic Gros, author of *A Philosophy of Walking*, wrote, "Walking is a matter not just of truth, but also of reality. To walk is to experience the real. Not reality as our physical exteriority or as what might count as a subject, but reality as what holds good: the principle of solidity, of resistance. When you walk you prove it with every step: the earth holds good. With every pace, the entire weight of my body finds support and rebounds, takes a spring. There is everywhere a solid base somewhere underfoot."[53] Gros emphasizes that walking anchors us in the real world as we are in our own thoughts, experiencing our own reality within nature.

It is well-documented that many creative people will engage in some kind of daily exercise. Beethoven took long, vigorous walks for at least two hours or more each day. He took a pencil and paper with him to write down any ideas that came to him during these daily walks. Author Victor Hugo, after writing all morning, took long walks on the beach daily.[54] Exercise should be part of your daily structure whether you do it before or after a bout of working. It is certainly a priority when you are on your retreat. You may want to take a walk or hike in nature before you sit down to meditate and go into deep thought.

You can walk briskly, or you can walk slowly. It is your choice. But you must get out into nature and walk for some period of time that will let you slip into your head—your mind— more fully. Many experts suggest that walking for thirty minutes a day at about three miles an hour, five days a week, is a good recommended amount of exercise.[55] Walking has a low impact on your overall body, and where you walk is completely up to you. Wherever you take your retreat, you can walk in a large central park in a more populated area, or if you are out in the country, have your pick of open fields or wooded areas.

The act of being outside, walking, and breathing in fresh air with the visual stimulations of the landscape around you will take your mind in new directions. Walking evokes thinking about those aspects of your life that you have been suppressing or avoiding; you can contemplate your goals, dreams, and visions of the future your imagination has crafted. You will see your mood improve, and your mind will be more open to creative thoughts. Going for a walk is the perfect primer, a requirement in my mind, for sitting down in a secluded spot and unleashing your imagination.

I'm not here to preach about improving your health through diet and exercise. I leave that to your partner or doctor. What I do want is for you to think about how best to optimize your personal retreat to maximize the benefits of thinking about your goals and laying out the plans to reach them. Eating well and exercising will simply contribute to the personal retreat experience.

It is important to give some thought and planning to what you will accomplish each day of your retreat without over-scheduling. It is all about finding that balance between doing too little or too much scheduling. This is tricky if you have a busy, structured day you adhere to with hour or half-hour meetings broken up by morning and afternoon breaks and an hour or so for lunch. We are often strivers to our appointment calendar and move through the day from one thing to the next with hardly a moment to think.

So, not having that schedule makes some people feel agitated, nervous, and lost. The main purpose of finding your happy place is to move beyond those feelings, and the easiest way is to still create a daily schedule for yourself but make it a very light one— say, a block of time in the morning and the afternoon. If you feel more comfortable writing it down, do it in your journal longhand. I would avoid creating your schedule digitally on a smartphone. The point is to unplug; having an alarm notification sound off while you are in deep thought defeats that purpose.

There is no hard and fast rule regarding how long you should sit in deep thought or meditation; it should be fluid and natural. It will be how long it needs to be, and you will receive the most benefits by letting it be an organic process.

On my retreats, I start my morning journaling before having a light breakfast. Then, I may sit and read an article or a book before heading to a favorite spot with my folding camp chair to sit for several hours. I may park a distance away and walk to my destination, getting in some exercise and taking in the beginning of the day. When I arrive at my spot, I'll set up my chair and then go for another walk along the shoreline, depending on whether or not the tide is out. Again, I am not looking at a schedule and saying, "Oh, it's 9:30— time to walk for an hour." No, that is not the way this works. You have to let yourself meander and flow as you wish with no set daily schedule other than the time you will sit in stillness and deep thought each day.

Changing your diet, exercising, and loosely following a flexible retreat schedule is the best kind of retreat. This will help get you centered and into a different headspace because you are upending your normal daily routine to spend time working solely on your own intentions, goals, and a plan to achieve them on a timeline that is comfortable for you.

Quick Tips:

1. Having a healthy mind and active imagination, along with a healthy body, means taking care of yourself with exercise and nutrition.
2. The simple act of walking is proven to be good cardio exercise. Walking lowers your stress level and gives you more energy while building stamina.
3. The act of being outside, walking, and breathing in fresh air with the visual stimulations of the landscape around you will take your mind in new directions.
4. It is well-documented that many creative people will engage in some kind of daily exercise.
5. There is no hard and fast rule as to how long you should sit in deep thought or meditation; it should be fluid and natural.

Worksheet:

Healthy Mind, Healthy Body Personal Retreat

Part 1: Setting Goals for a Healthy Mind

1. What specific mental health goals do you want to achieve during your personal retreat?

   _____

   _____

   _____

   _____

2. What activities or practices, such as meditation, journaling, or walking, will support your mental health goals?

   _____

   _____

   _____

   _____

3. How will you measure your progress toward achieving your mental health goals?

   _____

   _____

Part 2: Setting Goals for a Healthy Body

1. What specific physical health goals do you want to achieve during your personal retreat?

   _____

   _____

   _____

   _____

   _____

2. What activities or practices, such as yoga, hiking, or healthy eating, will support your physical health goals?

   _____

   _____

   _____

   _____

   _____

3. How will you measure your progress toward achieving your physical health goals?

   _____

   _____

Part 3: Creating a Schedule

1. Create a schedule that incorporates activities that support your mental and physical health goals.

    _____

    _____

    _____

    _____

    _____

    _____

2. Determine the best times of day for each activity based on your energy levels and other commitments.

    _____

    _____

    _____

    _____

3. Build in time for rest and relaxation, such as napping or taking a bath.

    _____

Part 4: Preparing Your Space

1. Create a clean, uncluttered space for your personal retreat.

   _____

   _____

2. Incorporate elements that support your mental and physical health, such as plants, natural lighting, or outdoors in nature.

   _____

   _____

Part 5: Nurturing Your Mind and Body

1. Engage in activities that support your mental and physical health goals, such as meditation or hiking.

   _____

   _____

2. Practice mindfulness throughout the day, such as eating mindfully or taking a break to stretch.

   _____

   _____

3. Make healthy food choices that support your physical health goals.

_____

_____

Part 6: Reflection

1. After your personal retreat, reflect on your mental and physical health goals.

_____

_____

_____

_____

_____

_____

_____

2. Review your progress toward achieving each goal and any insights or lessons you gained during your retreat.

_____

_____

_____

_____

_____

_____

_____

3. Consider how you can continue to nurture your mental and physical health in your daily life after your personal retreat.

_____

_____

_____

_____

_____

— ᴼ —

Remember, a healthy mind and body are essential for personal growth and development. Use this worksheet to help you set goals and create a schedule that supports your mental and physical health during your personal retreat.

— Step 6 —

YOUR ACTUAL RETREAT AND GETTING THE MOST OUT OF IT

Approximately a year after the birth of my eldest daughter, I found myself wanting some personal time amidst the demands of my professional career and family life. During this period, I decided to embark on a weeklong sailing course in a coastal region of Maine. Thankfully, my wife understood and supported my need for solitude, and thus, I enrolled in a Fundamentals of Sailing-1 program offered by a seasonal school nestled along the Maine coastline. When the anticipated moment arrived, I carefully packed my bags, bid farewell to my loved ones, and set off on my journey to Maine, eagerly anticipating the commencement of the sailing class and a week by myself.

It was early August, and in the northern reaches of Maine, the days are very long. The sun does not set until just past 8:00 PM, and the twilight sky, magic hour, lasts until after 9:00 PM. I didn't know anyone at the school or in the area, which allowed me to take a breather from constantly being on the go, doing things and talking with people. At that time, there was no Wi-fi at the facility, and I had to go to the top of a nearby hill to get any kind of cell phone reception. It was a remote place.

The sailing class started at 8:00 AM and lasted until 5:00 PM, with dinner at around 6:00 PM. Yes, the school made room and board available, making it much easier to attend. The class began on a Monday and was completed the following Friday afternoon. With the sun out late, I found myself sitting on the waterfront in the early evening, after a light dinner, staring out at the nautical scenery and the splendor of nature in full bloom.

There were several small uninhabited islands reasonably close to the coastline, and it was quiet except for the natural sounds around me. The lush emerald leaves rustled as a light breeze passed through the tree canopies above as I soaked in the view with the rhythmic lapping of water along the shoreline and the intermittent buzzing of crickets signaling the day was coming to an end. As the sun sank into the horizon, the sky became awash with warm reds and magentas, reddish oranges and yellows, like paint on a canvas. I walked back to my room.

I could actually be in my thoughts, and it was an almost alien feeling to me, but I noticed the effect that being alone like this was having on me. It was strange and wonderful at the same time. I had not experienced that before, not to this degree, or if I did, it was so long ago I'd forgotten what it was like to be in your own thoughts for hours uninterrupted. It was like that moment of amazement when you look at a night sky filled with stars for the first time away from the ambient lights of a metropolitan area. There is a sense of awe that brings a smile to your face when you first see it—that child-like wonder of discovery.

The first few days, I could actually feel the stress washing away. My shoulders, neck, and back became more relaxed, almost sore from the release of tension I had been carrying. I slept better than I had in a long while. Okay, let's face it: we had a newborn at home at the time, and of course, I slept well just being away on my own, but it was a deep, refreshing, and uninterrupted sleep. I found myself going to sleep quickly and without the usual tossing and turning and the restlessness I normally experienced before falling asleep because I was thinking about a million things at once. It was nearly incomprehensible that I could get seven to eight hours of sleep a night while I was in Maine taking that sailing class. Yet, that happened for the entire week, and it was an insightful feeling.

The area I was in was so rural that I found myself going to bed at 9:00 PM and sleeping straight through to 4:30 or 5:00 in the morning. If they had sidewalks, they would have rolled them up by early evening— it was that quiet. I woke up well-rested, had plenty of energy, and was more mentally alert throughout the day. There was no feeling of being tired or dragging around in the afternoon that was typical during my normal workweek. I repeated that daily routine of getting up early, showering, and taking a leisurely walk down to the small general store each morning before having breakfast. I resisted buying *The New York Times* or *The Wall Street Journal,* opting instead for the *Bangor Daily News.* I wanted to disconnect as much as I could but still be able to read a newspaper and have a minimal sense of what was going on in the outside world. This was before the proliferation of online additions, news alerts, and all the other distractions on all the electronic gadgets vying for our attention.

That was the first time I noticed the restful, restorative, and rejuvenating effect that taking some alone time had on my mental and physical well-being. There is voluminous research on the importance of just having a deep sleep. Sleep has been proven to improve memory recall, regulate metabolism, and reduce mental fatigue. When you sleep, the brain reorganizes and recharges itself while removing toxins that have accumulated throughout the day. This evidence demonstrates that sleeping can clear the brain and help maintain its normal functionality. Each phase of the sleep cycle restores and rejuvenates the brain for optimal function.[56] The fact that I was getting a full, deep sleep was evidenced by how refreshed I felt each morning. I journaled about it each day to track how I was feeling, what I was thinking about, and any significant thoughts or ideas that popped into my mind.

Experiencing such a restful night's sleep each evening for a week will make you realize how poorly you have been sleeping. It shows that we all get so used to how something is that it becomes the norm—it feels normal—even though it is not. Actually, having a real, proper sleep was revelatory for me, and I wanted to maintain it after experiencing it on what I view as my first retreat.

I realized during those initial years of taking my retreat that I no longer had fuzzy thinking or was easily distracted. My mind seemed more focused after getting a good night's sleep. That is no surprise since mounting evidence suggests that poor sleep can and does negatively affect your overall health. Research points to seven to eight hours of sleep as optimal for your health. Those who constantly get that amount of sleep appear to live longer, according to the research. But it is not just about the quantity of sleep but also the quality. Lower-quality sleep is associated with a host of health issues, including inflammation that can lead to obesity, diabetes, heart disease, and some cancers, as well as cognitive problems.[57]

—⁓—

Sidebar—
Techniques to Make Dreams More Productive While Sleeping

Our dreams can be powerful tools for creativity, problem-solving, and personal growth. By using a few simple techniques, you can make your dreams more productive and gain insights and ideas that can help you in your waking life.

During the Day:

Making dreams more productive during the day. Using the daytime hours to make your dreams more productive involves setting intentions and cultivating awareness of our subconscious mind. By reflecting on our experiences and emotions throughout the day, we can identify areas of our lives that may be affecting our dreams. Engaging in creative activities, such as writing or drawing, can also help stimulate our imagination and increase the likelihood of having vivid and productive dreams. Additionally, practicing mindfulness and relaxation techniques, such as meditation, can help to calm the mind and promote restful sleep, leading to more productive and meaningful dreams.

Before Bedtime:

Set an intention for your dreams. Before you go to bed, take a few moments to set an intention for what you want to dream about. This could be a problem you want to solve or a question you want to answer.

Avoid heavy meals or stimulating activities before bedtime. Eating a heavy meal or engaging in stimulating activities before bedtime can interfere with your sleep and dreams.

— ⟋⟍ —

While Sleeping:

Keep a dream journal by your bed. Keep a journal or notebook by your bed to record your dreams as soon as you wake up. This can help you remember your dreams and gain insights from them.

Practice lucid dreaming. Mnemonic induction of lucid dreams (MILD) is a technique used to induce lucid dreaming, which is the ability to become aware that you are dreaming and take control of your dream. The MILD technique involves setting an intention to remember that you are dreaming while in the dream state. This is done through a combination of reality checks, such as looking at your hands, and visualization exercises, such as imagining yourself becoming lucid in a dream. By practicing the MILD technique regularly, individuals may increase their likelihood of having lucid dreams and gaining insights and inspiration from their dreams.

— ◌ —

After You Wake Up:

Record your dreams in your dream journal. Write down as many details as you can remember about your dream, including any emotions or sensations you experienced.

Reflect on your dream. Consider the symbolism and themes of your dream and how they might relate to your waking life. Think about any insights or ideas you gained from your dream.

Take action on your insights. Use the insights and ideas gained from your dream to solve problems, make decisions, or pursue new opportunities.

— ◌ —

Remember, our dreams can be a powerful tool for personal growth and creativity. Use these techniques to make your dreams more productive and gain insights and ideas to help you in your waking life.

Experiencing deep sleep during a week-long personal retreat was enough to convince me that having time to myself was eye-opening, especially in terms of how I was leading my life and how I should be living it. I was working a daily grind and didn't realize just how much my body was conditioned to the exhaustion, sleep deprivation, stress, poor diet, and low energy that became the norm in my life. The daily treadmill of getting up tired, going to work, stressing over deadlines, eating at the desk or on the run, battling rush-hour traffic, getting home to family, and other obligations was wearing down my mind and body. That never became so clear to me than on these early retreats.

I wondered what I could do to improve my sleep patterns at home for the rest of the year between retreats. Could I actually make the necessary changes to keep that refreshed and recharged feeling I had during my personal retreat? I looked at all aspects of my daily routine to see what adjustments I could make that would improve my health. I looked at those habits that form subconsciously without you even knowing they are happening—habits like when I went to bed, how much television I watched before sleeping, and how much caffeine I ingested during the day. What little things could I do to make changes to improve my sleep?

The restorative effects of sleeping were just the beginning of my journey. Over several years of taking my personal retreats, I began formulating a plan that became routine during subsequent retreats. As I observed and learned new things, I made notes and adjustments, improving my own life process year in and year out. Making small adjustments to your lifestyle can have dramatic impacts on your well-being. Just not drinking any caffeinated beverages after noon each day did wonders for helping me fall asleep quicker and be less restless in bed.

One of the benefits of being in a rural place and unplugging from all the gadgets and media distractions is that you can get healthier sleep just from being exposed to natural light patterns, going to sleep not long after the sun sets and waking up at dawn. It also helped not having a television and limiting the screen time on devices. The emissive screen light of computers, cell phones, tablets, and televisions has negative effects on your sleep patterns. The devices emit blue light, which is disruptive to the production of melatonin, the hormone that controls our natural circadian rhythm or sleep cycle. Taking a cue from my experience of unplugging and not having a television on the retreat, I looked at reducing my use of gadgets in the evening. Not using any devices thirty to forty minutes before bed helped me transition my body to sleep.[58] All of these little steps added up to a much more restful night's sleep.

I believe it's important for your mind and body to focus on sleeping well while on your personal retreat. When you experience the regenerative effects of quality sleep, you will start to experience your life differently in how you feel, think, and view the world and your particular situation.

If the first thing needed for a successful retreat is sleep, then the next item on your list should be time set aside for stillness. What I mean by stillness is not being completely motionless but being in the moment alone in a place with little or no distractions. I prefer complete solitude with nothing but nature around me. Being completely alone is terrifying for some people. We have become so connected through email, text, and the various social media platforms that the thought of being without a smartphone or laptop, even for a day, would make some feel lost, agitated, and out of touch. Some cannot go for even an hour or more without checking the likes on their Facebook page or seeing who added to their story on Instagram. I cannot stress it enough— spending time alone on your retreat is critically important. There is nothing to be terrified of by being alone for a period of time. You'll quickly realize that those fears of missing out will be replaced with a sense of accomplishment in thinking through your goals.

As important as it is to be social and interact with others, it is equally important to be alone. Having unstructured time by yourself is not only healthy but necessary. Being alone allows us to decompress, process, and simply have no pressure to do anything other than whatever is desired. This will aid in helping you to understand your sense of self, what you truly are interested in, and what you want to do. It will also give you the opportunity to develop who you actually are as an individual and not just what others want you to be. Alone time is an opportunity to discover new ideas and interests that can help give you new insights into your life.[59] Spending time alone will boost your confidence, productivity, and creativity.

To be clear, I am talking about taking alone time for yourself, not loneliness. These are two different things. Having alone time is just that, being alone with your thoughts, undistracted and in solitude. This is the time you take away from your normal everyday social relationships. Having regular social relationships has a positive effect on mental health, physical health, and mortality risks. Studies on mortality have shown that "individuals with the lowest level of involvement in social relationships are more likely to die than those with greater involvement."[60] Human beings are social animals, and many of these scientific studies have shown that the quantity and quality of our relationships impact health. There is a definite delineation between our ability to choose to take time alone in solitude for the purposes of self-examination and that of a constant feeling of loneliness.

Loneliness is a condition that is associated with weakened immune systems, heart disease, and depression.[61] If you are experiencing loneliness and depression, you should seek out professional medical help. Loneliness and the negative side effects that accompany it are not to be taken lightly, and you should not be ashamed or embarrassed by it. Many people suffer from these symptoms; it is part of the human condition. They require your immediate attention, and the best place to start is with your doctor. Your doctor will be able to advise you with solid referrals to get the necessary help you need to get at the root cause of your loneliness and onto a path of resolving the underlying issues. There is a clear distinction between loneliness and being alone that you must differentiate between for your own well-being.

For the purposes of this book, I am discussing being alone for the specific motivation of self-reflection and self-improvement. It is about scheduling alone time or *me time* for yourself in relation to your personal retreat. This will positively impact your life, including enhancing your creative expression, benefiting your brain and cognitive function, increasing self-awareness, and improving your relationships through thought and reflection.[62] Each topic has positive benefits to being alone but not feeling lonely. I am firm in my belief that spending time alone on a regular basis and sitting in stillness with your thoughts will have a profound and everlasting change in your life.

Quick Tips:

1. Experiencing a restful night's sleep each evening for a week will make you realize how poorly you have been sleeping.
2. One of the benefits of being in a rural place and unplugging from all the gadgets and media distractions is that you can get healthier sleep just from being exposed to natural light patterns.
3. Stillness is not about being completely motionless but being in the moment alone in a place with little or no distractions.
4. There is nothing to be terrified of by being alone for a period of time.

5. Loneliness is a condition that is associated with weakened immune systems, heart disease, and depression. If you are experiencing loneliness and depression, you should seek out professional medical help immediately.

6. Being alone is for the specific motivation of self-reflection and self-improvement. It is about scheduling alone time or *me-time* for yourself.

Worksheet:
Getting the Most Out of Your Retreat

Part 1: Creating Your Retreat Space

1. Set up your retreat space to create a relaxing and conducive environment for you to be undistracted and have the ability to think deeply.

_____

_____

_____

_____

2. Remove any distractions or items that may interfere with the focus and concentration necessary for deep sleep and positive dreaming.

_____

_____

_____

3. Spend time in a location that will allow you to practice stillness and meditation.

_____

_____

_____

Part 2: Engaging in Activities

1. Engage in journaling during waking hours, and write down your dreams when you wake from a restful sleep.

_____

_____

_____

_____

_____

_____

_____

2. Create a schedule or routine to help you stay on track with your activities.

_____

_____

_____

_____

_____

3. Take breaks as needed to rest and recharge.

_____

_____

Part 3: Reflecting on Your Experience

1. Take time each day to reflect on your experiences and progress toward your goals.

_____

_____

2. Journal or record your thoughts, dreams, and insights to help you process your experience.

_____

_____

_____

_____

3. Use your reflections to adjust your activities and goals as needed.

_____

_____

_____

Part 4: Following Through on Your Intentions

1. Create an action plan for following through on your insights, dreams, and intentions gained during the retreat.

_____

_____

_____

_____

_____

_____

2. Identify any support or resources you may need to implement your plan.

_____

_____

_____

_____

3. Set a timeline for completing each action step and hold yourself accountable.

_____

_____

_____

_____

Part 5: Reflection

1. After your retreat, reflect on your overall experience and progress toward your goals.

_____

_____

_____

_____

2. Consider any insights or lessons you gained during your retreat that can help you continue to grow and develop.

_____

_____

_____

_____

3. Use your reflections to create a plan for integrating your insights and intentions into your daily life.

_____

_____

_____

_____

———⌒———

Remember, a personal retreat can be a transformative experience that can help you recharge, reflect, and reconnect with yourself. Use this worksheet to help you prepare for your retreat, create your retreat space, engage in activities that align with your goals, reflect on your experiences, and follow through on your intentions.

— Step 7 —

CREATIVE THINKING

Based on my personal experiences, I can attest to the profound impact that embarking on an annual personal retreat to my cherished haven has had on my creativity, resulting in an enhanced creative output. Extensive research also reveals that many of history's most imaginative thinkers dedicated ample time to their craft or profession in solitude. Visionaries such as physicists Albert Einstein and Isaac Newton primarily worked in seclusion, often engaging with others' ideas indirectly by delving into their colleagues' research papers and books. Similarly, the renowned composer Wolfgang Amadeus Mozart, celebrated for his remarkable body of over six hundred compositions, found solace and inspiration in moments of complete solitude. As he eloquently expressed, "When I am, as it were, completely myself, entirely alone, and of good cheer... it is on such occasions that my ideas flow best and most abundantly." The influential Spanish painter and co-founder of the Cubism movement, Pablo Picasso, firmly believed that "without great solitude, no serious work is possible." The Pulitzer Prize-winning poet and author Carl Sandburg observed that "one of the greatest necessities in America is to discover creative solitude."[63]

These testimonies from accomplished individuals further

emphasize the transformative power of solitude in fostering creativity and its indispensable role in producing meaningful and groundbreaking work.

The list of notable artists, scientists, and thinkers is deep and varied, with the common thread of advocating for alone time to help get them to the peak of their creativity. Much has been written about creativity, including a 1959 essay by author and professor Isaac Asimov, which I read many years ago and found inspiring. Asimov writes, "My feeling is that as far as creativity is concerned, isolation is required. The creative person is, in any case, continually working at it. His mind is shuffling his information at all times, even when he is not conscious of it."[64] Asimov went on to observe that "the presence of others can only inhibit this process, since creation is embarrassing. For every new good idea you have, there are a hundred, ten thousand foolish ones, which you naturally do not care to display."[65] Animation director and artist Chuck Jones famously said, "Every artist has thousands of bad drawings in them and the only way to get rid of them is to draw them out."[66] As an artist, it is much better to create alone so that you are uninhibited in your expression and exploration, however good or terrible the creations may be.

The creative thought process is much different when we are alone from our regular every day thinking about tasks and to-do lists. When we sit alone in our own thoughts, with no distractions from the outside world, we can engage in what is called "meta-cognition," which means "awareness or analysis of one's own learning or thinking processes."[67] This is the ability to think beyond ourselves and our everyday social roles. We can sit and reflect on a single topic or goal and do so with fresh perspectives and insights just by being alone.

Solitude allows us to analyze our thoughts and find new approaches or ideas we might not have thought about before. Once a new idea, intention, or goal develops, we have to fully form that idea by visualizing it to make it actionable. In other words, write it down with associated notes so you can create an achievable plan to bring it to fruition. That is one of the reasons you should always have a journal handy, not just on your retreat, but all the time to write down ideas that pop into your mind.

The act of being alone lets you depart from your normal routine, which in turn has the benefit of letting you think differently. Think of it this way: each day, you do some of the same tasks, like driving to work, that become so repetitive over time that you are on autopilot. How many times have you gotten home and thought that was fast? I just left work, and now I'm home, and I don't really remember much of the journey. It's because you have done it so many times that your brain goes on autopilot, and you think about other things. But, if you decided to take another route home each day, you would be more in the moment of driving, paying attention to where you are going so that you would remember the journey. A different route lets you see sights along that journey for the first time.

Every day, you leave for home around the same time and get to work at about the same time, likely pulling into the same parking spot, getting your cup of tea or coffee, and then going through some standard routine throughout your workday. The personal retreat breaks that routine and makes you do different things, which may include trying something you have not done before. This allows you to get out of that daily grind of being on autopilot and start thinking differently about everything you are doing during each day of your retreat. Your brain is engaged, active, and stimulated, which leads to more creative thoughts. Mixing up what you do daily will mix up how you look at what you do, leading to more creative thinking and insights.

A good example of this is to rotate your daily routines much the way farmers rotate their crops to keep the soil fertile. Changing up routines and rotating your tasks gives you a sharper focus and heightened cognitive function. This will allow your mind to be more alert and receptive to new ideas, ways of looking, and creative problem-solving.

During my personal retreats, I always experience this sense of new ideas and the way I look at the world because I break away from those daily routines. Doing something completely different by being alone in a new environment has immediately affected my thinking process and creative output. This can also be achieved outside the retreat by simply taking a break. The act of getting up and going for a walk will get the blood circulating and help reinvigorate your mind.

Taking a walk at lunchtime or during a morning or afternoon break each day breaks up long stretches of concentration and helps clear our minds, which in turn makes us more creative.

Being alone lets me reflect on what I want and not what others may expect me to reflect on. We are all influenced by those we associate with who are around us regularly. At work, this is known as groupthink, which is the practice of thinking or making decisions as a group in a way that discourages creativity or individual responsibility.[68] This may or may not be true at your place of work, but I believe that people are influenced by those around them no matter the situation, and that can stifle fresh ideas.

How often have you been in a meeting when the boss says something and everyone agrees, but you find yourself thinking, "This is crazy" or "That's a bad idea," yet no one speaks up? Outside of your job, you may have experienced peer pressure when you are pushed into doing what the group wants rather than what you want. Just think back to when you were in grade school. We have all experienced peer pressure at one time or another during those years. It didn't end at grade school; the peer pressure and bullying then carried through to college and into your work life. The personal retreat allows you to get far away from those toxic social pressures.

I can remember being in meetings at work with a manager mentioned earlier and hearing him say something that was just simply a bad idea. Everyone else in the meeting nodded in agreement, and I just thought to myself, "This is not a good idea." I made an alternative suggestion and got a look that said, "Shut up, I'm the boss, and only I get to come up with creative ideas." A few people started to react positively but then retracted their support based on the reaction from the manager. It was an example of bullying, toxic peer pressure, and the groupthink dynamic in all its glory.

When you are alone on a retreat, there is no groupthink or peer pressure. No one is there to bully you into doing anything you don't want. You can be yourself, be who you are and want to be, and reflect on what you want without being tainted, bullied, or pressured. You can think about whatever you want to think about and lose your inhibitions because there is no one to impress, influence, or judge you in any way. You can laugh out loud, talk to yourself, cry, or even scream in the woods at the top of your lungs if you want to. Being alone will let you be more in touch with your own feelings, desires, and dreams. That alone time will give you a clearer mind to think about what makes you unique and what creativity you have to contribute. All these thoughts will flow through your thinking and spark many ideas. That time by yourself will open you up to looking at your intentions for the retreat in a different light you would not otherwise have thought of with the distractions of your everyday life. This is part of the imaginative thinking you will experience taking your own personal retreat and why it is important to your well-being.

We are all creative. I know some will disagree with that statement, but we all have the same creative abilities; some just develop and take their creativity much further than others because they work at it. If you had spent every day practicing the violin five or six hours a day, you would have become accomplished at playing that instrument. The same is true if you went to a figure drawing class three times a week; you would become reasonably good at drawing the human form over time. And the same goes for writing every day. Eventually, your writing will improve, and you will develop your own writing "voice." That is true, of course, of any endeavor if you are encouraged, taught, and inspired to succeed at it.

How often have you been told, "No, you can't do that," or "That's a dumb idea," or even, "That's not how you do that?" From the earliest ages, we have been conditioned and influenced by friends, parents, siblings, or teachers on whether we can or can't do certain things. We are often discouraged from putting our creative ideas to use because others view them as impractical, different, or "not how things are done." Yet, history has shown that many have broken through those negative vibes and let their creativity soar. Look at inventors and visionaries like Thomas Edison, Louis Pasteur, Steve Jobs, Elon Musk, and others who persevered. Why? Because they have allowed themselves to spend time alone with their thoughts and ideas. They gave themselves permission to engage in their creativity, which is what the personal retreat will do for you if you are willing to step out of your comfort zone and find your own happy place that you can travel to where you can think clearly and with purpose.

Creativity involves using your imagination, which is simply the formation of new ideas, images, and concepts—the visualization in your mind—of things that don't presently exist in the real world. The imagination is the part of your brain that can visualize or invent new things not currently perceived by your senses. Everyone has the ability to use their own imagination. The imagination manifests, in varying degrees, differently in various people, with some having more highly developed imaginations than others. Your imagination makes it possible to experience an object, work of art, or whole world within your mind.[69] It is like when you daydream and see yourself as a superhero or doing something physically impossible for you to do, you are imagining it in your mind's eye. You are seeing it vividly in all its details.

We all use our imagination through our dreams, nightmares, daydreaming during waking hours, and the ability to visualize. We have the ability to dream of the most fantastical things while we are sleeping, but many rarely remember what they dreamt. Yet, others remember more, have more lucid dreams, and are disciplined enough to write down the details or even the crux of a dream when they wake up. Often, people daydream about being someone or creating something incredible only to chalk it up to silliness or being impractical. The reality is that some of the best ideas have come out of people letting their imagination run wild while dreaming or daydreaming.

Your imagination can let you travel to distant places without limitations. The act of visualization is one in which you use your imagination to form images or a scene in your mind and act out or create those things only you can imagine. Listening to music, I have envisioned myself playing guitar and singing on stage in front of a stadium-size audience as I sing along to the song. We have all seen someone play "air guitar" as they listen to music, which is that individual imagining that they are in the band or on stage performing. A retreat gives you the ability to do this for long stretches of time. We all have imagined ourselves as any number of people or doing any number of things. We think to ourselves, "If I were in charge, I would do …," or "If I were running the company…"

Your imagination is not limited to only seeing pictures or movies in your mind's eye but can also include your five senses. You can imagine sounds like nature or music, taste flavors, smell scents, feel textures, and even experience emotions, sometimes overwhelmingly physical sensations. Have you ever woken up and sworn that you smelled something, felt a touch, or thought you heard something, and none of it was real but only imagined?

Using your imagination, whether dreaming or daydreaming, can provide a degree of stress relief and calmness. It can give you a momentary sense of sadness or happiness. Using your imagination while on your retreat is a vital addition to the experience of finding your happy place. You will be able to thoroughly imagine the positive outcomes of your intentions while sitting in a meditative state in deep thought. Being able to sit in a secluded spot and allow your imagination free reign to visualize anything and everything you want is part of the purpose of the personal retreat and finding your happy place in this world. Once your mind is free to imagine anything you want, you may even develop your imagination further than you thought possible.

We have all heard of "think positive." Well, there is truth to that phrase when it is applied to achieving those things you want in life. Norman Vincent Peale, the minister and author who popularized the concept of positive thinking, said, "If you paint in your mind a picture of bright and happy expectations, you put yourself into a condition conducive to your goal."[70] He advocated that you use your mind's ability to create positive imagery, to imagine the outcome of whatever it is you want. To thoroughly live, create, and visualize your dreams and goals in your mind. By repeating this process, you have subconsciously planted the seeds of success in your mind. If you repeat this action enough, you will start to distill the solutions and actions needed for the intentions you wrote down prior to leaving on your retreat. Think about that for a moment. You create the positive imagery in your mind to influence the outcome of whatever you want to accomplish.

When I am on my annual retreat, I engage my imagination often throughout each day. I am comfortable sitting in a quiet place and thinking, sometimes imagining some of the wildest, craziest things and making myself laugh out loud. I also allow myself to sit in wonder or just have a great, actionable idea. This is all part of the process of engaging your imagination. You have to get to your happy place and just let your imagination take off to wherever it wants to go.

If you work on the left side, the analytical side, of your brain all the time, it will take some time for you to develop the process. But you can do it if you grant yourself permission and the alone time needed to develop the right side, the creative side, of your brain. Many people who consider themselves "non-creative" struggle with this idea of using their imagination, but like anything in life, it can be learned and developed.

The repeated visualization of solving a problem or reaching a goal is part of using your imagination positively. Sitting in a quiet place each day, closing your eyes, and seeing yourself solving a work-related issue or formulating a picture in your mind of yourself reaching a goal will plant the seeds in your subconscious mind needed to achieve those desires. Peale famously said, "repetition of the same thought or physical action develops into a habit which, repeated frequently enough, becomes an automatic reflex."[71] In other words, if you can think it, you can make it happen.

"All our dreams can come true if we have the courage to pursue them," Walt Disney said.[72] Pursuing your dreams begins in your mind and your imagination, which only you are in charge of. No one else can control your thought process unless you let them.

Conversely, if you don't understand the inherent power of your imagination, you will likely expect the worst or just allow situations to play out with no control or input from you. Negative thinking feeds on itself and is something you must get into the habit of putting out of your thought process. This is where some people just don't have the wherewithal to change. They view their life as one they have no control over, and they continue to think negative thoughts of, "I'm not good enough," "I didn't go to the right school," "I don't have the pedigree of this person or that person." This is exactly the type of thinking you have to put out of your mind all the time, especially during the retreat. It is why you have to take the retreat solo, with no one and nothing to influence your thoughts. You can then have complete control in keeping negative thoughts out of your mind and only dwell on *positive* ones.

In 1929, Albert Einstein said in an interview that "imagination is more important than knowledge. For knowledge is limited, whereas imagination embraces the entire world, stimulating progress, giving birth to evolution."[73] It is the imagination that has led to all the great discoveries of the world. Bold thinkers create great works of art, discover cures to diseases, invent new things so life is infinitely better or sometimes worse, and devise whole new industries that have changed the world with a positive effect on humanity. These achievements have sprung from the imagination of individuals like you and me.

It was important to me to understand the imagination and how it works. This is another purpose of the personal retreat: to find the answers to our intentions, desires, and goals through the use of our imagination as applied to the knowledge we already possess. Imagination is the key to finding your happy place on your personal retreat. It is the power that fuels the creativity we need to elevate ourselves to greatness. It is the engine that drives us to achieve our goals and live the life we want to live, not one that others want us to live.

Accessing our imagination is easier when alone, away from devices and routines. Regularly doing so is key to changing and improving your life. During my personal retreat, I spend a week using my imagination to generate ideas and set goals. I ask questions like where I see myself in two and five years, allowing my mind to roam freely without judgment. Every idea deserves consideration. Another question: What do I need for happiness, free from obstacles? Reflecting on these questions alone provides clarity.

Overcoming obstacles to reach goals requires deep contemplation over time. Satisfaction upon reaching a goal may be fleeting; be ready to set new ones to avoid "buyer's remorse." Strive for something new, big or small, to keep your mind sharp and creativity flowing.

The imagination is the thrust that will propel us toward our goals if we have the drive, motivation, and belief in ourselves. Knowing the various types of imagination and how each type interacts with one another allowed me to feel more at ease with the process of letting my imagination run free.

The Eight Types of Imagination

When you are in your happy place, you will be able to use your imagination in a whole "variety of cognitive processes, including planning, hypothetical reasoning, picturing things in the past or the future, comprehending language, and, of course, in design and creativity in engineering and the arts."[74] That process begins with you sitting in a quiet, secluded place where you can be undisturbed for as long as is necessary to think deeply about your intentions.

Our imagination enables us to create new meanings from cognitive cues or stimuli within the environment, which, on occasion, can lead to new insights[75]. Eight documented types of imagination have been explored in scientific research.

The first is known as *effectuative imagination*. It is where your imagination synthesizes new concepts and ideas. This is the birth or embryonic stage of your idea forming, the raw state. It's often incomplete and needs more thought, more information, which will come with further reflection. This type of imagination is flexible. It permits continuous change and leads the way toward other forms of your imagination. The effectuative imagination is where "entrepreneurial planning, strategy crafting, particularly in opportunity construction, development, and assembling all the necessary resources required to exploit any opportunity."[76] This phase of the imagination will give you the *seed* or *crumbs* of an idea you can run with and start to shape into whatever it will be. Think of it like a sculptor pushing around clay, adding some here and taking away from there, as they mold their work of art.

This leads to the *intellectual* or *constructive imagination*, which is about taking all these various pieces of information, those crumbs, and thinking about their collective meanings. We use the constructive imagination when considering and developing a theory from different pieces of information or pondering various issues of meaning, say in the areas of philosophy, management, politics, etc. This constructive imagination "originates from a definite idea or plan and thus is guided imagination as it has a distinct purpose which in the end must be articulated after a period of painstaking and sometimes meticulous endeavor."[77] This is a conscious process that can take varying degrees of time to sort out, often during periods of intense thought and other times with little or no thought to the problem. It is also a process that allows the mind to wander into other forms of imagination, which then enable new insights and the development of other new concepts. It is the process of connecting the dots, so to speak.

That takes us into the *imaginative fantasy*, which helps us to create and develop stories, poems, screenplays, artwork, and immersive worlds, among many other creative examples that don't yet exist. Imaginative fantasy has been used by marketers to create a sense of fantasy for consumers that allows them to imagine themselves wearing a new pair of shoes or driving the hot new sports car. Those commercials create a seductive, idyllic image that the consumer can imagine themselves being a part of—they can project themselves into the situation where they are using the item being advertised. The imaginative fantasy constructs imagined and immersive worlds that don't exist for viewers to feel what it would be like to have the new product being marketed.

We are exposed to imaginative fantasy all around us all the time. Imaginative fantasy also allows us to create our own world in our minds, fantasize what it would be like to have great success, overcome a problem, be in a new job, or get a promotion at work. Imaginative fantasy can be a mixture of guided and unguided imagination and is important to artists, writers, dancers, musicians, and other people creating art and entertainment.[78]

While you are using your imagination, you may experience the next phase: *empathy* for others who may have a connection to your intentions. Empathy imagination helps a person know emotionally what others are experiencing from their frame of reference. This allows our mind "to detach itself from one's self" and see the world from someone else's feelings, emotions, pain, and reasoning. This applies to those in our lives, like our family, friends, co-workers, or boss. Empathy allows us to feel what others are feeling and connect more fully with others. It enables us to join and understand each other better through interpersonal relationships. Empathy is used in marketing and branding to establish a connection with potential customers by appealing to their emotions, self-identity, and aspirations.[79] It is that ability to tap into the gap between your ambitions and the reality of achieving your goal—where you are and where you want to be.

Next is the *strategic imagination*, which is concerned with the vision of "what could be," the ability to recognize and evaluate opportunities by turning them into mental scenarios. Your imagination engages in connecting the dots to see and comprehend a collection of separate pieces of information that others may not see. This area of imagination is responsible for the "what if" or "what could be" scenarios we often formulate when thinking about our goals. It is the ability to recognize an opportunity that might not be overtly evident on the surface. The arbitrageur, a type of investor who attempts to profit from market inefficiencies, uses their strategic imagination to take pricing information from different markets to buy and sell securities, thereby yielding them a profit from the price spread between the different markets.

According to researchers, entrepreneurs spot particular opportunities and extrapolate potential achievable scenarios within the limits of their skills and ability to gather resources to exploit the opportunity.[80] This combines strategic thinking, visualization, and creativity to think through multiple scenarios and outcomes. The ability to look at the different scenarios from various vantage points will allow for objective evaluation and calculated risk-taking to be formulated.

Emotional imagination "is concerned with manifesting emotional dispositions and extending them into emotional scenarios." Imagination is necessary for emotions to exist and show up as feelings, moods, and attitudes. When we imagine things that scare us, we experience fear. When we imagine things that we find repulsive, we feel hate. And when we imagine troubling scenarios, we worry and feel anxious. Our beliefs and values are "developed through giving weight to imaginative scenarios that generate further sets of higher order emotions."[81] This is one of the most powerful forms of imagination and can easily dominate our thought process.[82] People spend vast amounts of time imagining the worst outcomes for a situation, which in turn makes them anxious, moody, or depressed. Often, those thoughts never materialize, though our emotional imagination has no end to creating them.

We have all experienced *dreams*, which is our unconscious imagination at work while we sleep. We experience images, ideas, emotions, and various sensations while in a state of sleep. Dreams show that every concept in our mind has its own psychic associations and that ideas we deal with in everyday life are by no means as precise as we think.[83] Dreams are a pathway, a connection, to our unconscious imagination and are subjective in the interpretation of what they mean. In his book, *The Interpretation of Dreams*, Sigmund Freud suggested that dreams are related to our desires or wish fulfillment.[84] In other words, it is a way for your subconscious mind to help you solve problems through the use of imagery and events or to give you clues needed to solve those issues.

I often focus on an issue or a problem just before going to

sleep, and many times, I will wake the next morning with an answer. This may simply involve thinking about your issue or asking yourself a question related to solving a matter before retiring for the evening. While you sleep, your subconscious mind works on a solution. Ernest Hemingway, author of *The Sun Also Rises* and *The Old Man and the Sea*, used to stop writing for the day mid-sentence, and no doubt his subconscious mind was at work on what the rest of the passage might be the next day. Many creative individuals use this practice either consciously or subconsciously.[85]

Finally, that brings us to the eighth type of imagination, *memory reconstruction*, which is the process of memory retrieval of people, objects, and events. Our memory is formed from previous information consisting of a mixture of truth and belief, which is influenced by our feelings. Memory is additionally reconstructed to suit our beliefs into our own current read of the planet and the environment around us and thus is incredibly selective. This is why eyewitnesses to a crime or other events will have varying descriptions and details. The method of memory reconstruction happens inside our subconscious rising into our consciousness while not being very well tuned into what's reality and what's belief.[86]

Memory reconstruction is assimilation, and the mind may construct new information from random facts, beliefs, and experiences, which can result in a particular insight. This also manifests itself in how we may react to viewing a piece of art. The image resonates with random pieces of memory and can create any number of feelings or reactions based on our own beliefs, experiences, and attitudes. That is why different images evoke different emotional reactions in different people. Hence the expression, "beauty is in the eye of the beholder."

These eight different aspects of the imagination often overlap and may operate concurrently. Imaginative thinking provides the power to maneuver toward objectives and/or go on selected pathways. The imagination can move freely across fields and disciplines, whereas left brain or more logical thinking is oriented on a narrowly focused path. From this perspective, imagination is probably more important than knowledge, as knowledge without application is useless, as Einstein had so aptly observed. Many people are filled with knowledge but can't do anything with it other than regurgitating facts. Our imagination is what enables us to apply knowledge in new ways.[87]

I sit for hours during my retreats doing nothing but thinking, imagining, and visualizing the solutions or outcomes to my intentions, goals, and the many questions I ask myself. It may be an entire morning of sitting in a mindfulness state and meditating on one question, problem, or goal I wish to get clarity on. Thinking deeply about one topic or intention for three or four hours is not uncommon. It is possible I will not have a clear answer in that one session, and it will percolate in the back of my mind while I go off to do something else. It may require a few days of daydreaming and staring at the natural beauty around my happy place to get to a reasonable answer or idea. Eventually, the answer will emerge and show itself.

When I worked as a professional artist, I'd receive assignments and thoroughly discuss them with the director for clarity. Then, I'd visualize that task in my office, closing my eyes to imagine every detail, an integral part of my creative process. Before crafting any art, I had to envision it meticulously. The same applies to my writing; I ponder the topic, initiate the work, and write. For me, creativity flows, whether in thought or action.

The real essence of the retreat is reflection on and using your imagination to visualize your intentions, goals, and action plans: past, present, and future. Each year, I look back at what has transpired over the last twelve months since my previous retreat. Did I follow through on the goals and the actionable plans I set? This will be self-evident by the results of achieving those goals over the past year. You have to be honest with yourself. There is no one sitting there with you, no one judging you. An honest assessment will ultimately account for all your successes, failures, and progress.

The Find Your Happy Place retreat is based on a simple process: mindfully reflect on the past year's goals and events. Assess what worked and what didn't, embracing successes and setbacks as learning opportunities. Failure is a crucial step toward success, exemplified by Thomas Edison's three thousand lightbulb tests. I view setbacks and failures positively, recognizing them as steppingstones to my goals and a chance for valuable insights during my retreat.

Quick Tips:

1. Research has shown that some of the most creative thinkers in history also spent a lot of quality time working at their craft or profession alone.
2. Have a definite idea of what you want.
3. Sitting in stillness and focusing on your breathing to get into a meditative state only requires a place where you can be undisturbed for a specific amount of time that you determine.

Worksheet:
Creative Thinking Incorporating the Eight Types of Imagination on a Personal Retreat

Part 1: Indentifying Your Creative Goal

1. Identify the specific goal or challenge you want to focus your imagination on during your personal retreat.

_____

_____

_____

_____

2. Determine how each of the eight types of imagination can support your creative goal.

_____

_____

_____

_____

_____

_____

_____

3. Choose one or more types of imagination to focus on during your retreat.

_____

_____

Part 2: Engaging in Activities that Stimulate Creative Thinking

1. Engage in activities that stimulate your imagination, such as drawing, painting, or writing, and imagine what success looks like.

_____

_____

_____

_____

2. Incorporate activities that encourage divergent thinking, such as brainstorming or mind mapping.

_____

_____

_____

_____

_____

3. Take breaks to rest and recharge, and engage in activities that bring you joy and inspiration.

_____

_____

Part 3: Reflecting on Your Creative Thinking

1. Reflect on your creative thinking process and the insights or ideas you have generated using your imagination.

_____

_____

_____

_____

_____

2. Use your reflections to refine your ideas, identify any potential roadblocks or challenges, and imagine what success looks like.

_____

_____

_____

_____

_____

3. Determine any action steps needed to implement your ideas and achieve your creative goal.

_____

_____

_____

_____

_____

Part 4: Expanding Your Creative Thinking

1. Challenge yourself to engage with all eight types of imagination to generate new insights and perspectives.

   _____

   _____

   _____

   _____

   _____

   _____

   _____

2. Engage in activities that stimulate each type of imagination, such as visiting art galleries or exploring new environments.

   _____

   _____

3. Practice visualization exercises to help you generate new ideas and perspectives.

   _____

   _____

Part 5: Implementing Your Creative Ideas

1. Create an action plan for implementing your creative ideas.

   _____

   _____

   _____

   _____

   _____

   _____

2. Identify any support or resources you may need to achieve your
   creative goal.

   _____

   _____

   _____

   _____

   _____

3. Set a timeline for completing each action step and hold yourself
   accountable.

   _____

   _____

_____

_____

Part 6: Reflection

1. After your personal retreat, reflect on your overall experience and the ideas you generated using your imagination.

_____

_____

_____

_____

_____

_____

_____

2. Consider any insights or lessons you gained during your retreat that can help you continue using your imagination to think creatively in your daily life.

_____

_____

_____

_____

_____

3. Use your reflections to create a plan for implementing your creative ideas and continuing to expand your thinking using all eight types of imagination.

_____

_____

_____

_____

_____

_____

— ◡ —

Remember, creativity is a powerful tool for personal growth and development, and incorporating all eight types of imagination can help you generate new insights and perspectives. Use this worksheet to help you identify your creative goal, engage in activities that stimulate your chosen type(s) of imagination, reflect on your creative thinking, expand your thinking using your imagination, implement your creative ideas, and reflect on your overall experience.

— Step 8 —

VISUALIZATION

In the preceding chapter, I delved into the intertwined nature of imagination and visualization. Considerable literature exists on the positive impacts of visualization, yet I have come across numerous individuals who remain oblivious to its power or hold skeptical views regarding its benefits. Surprisingly, I have observed countless people engaging in negative visualization daily, inadvertently creating a life they do not desire. It is disheartening to witness how individuals employ visualization to conjure the worst possible outcomes, needlessly expending precious time worrying about the future and the potential negative consequences of their imaginings. Take a moment to reflect on a personal experience when excessive worry consumed you, perhaps fearing failure in an upcoming school exam to the point where it became a self-fulfilling prophecy. The act of fixating on failure, visualizing yourself falling short, unknowingly set in motion the very outcome you dreaded. You inadvertently manifested what you didn't want but intensely believed would transpire—failure. We can avoid this excessive worry and fixation on failure by shifting our focus to visualization. Visualization possesses the extraordinary ability to influence events, often tilting the scale toward either positive or negative outcomes.

Visualization is not used only by highly successful people or those who went to the "right" school or came from the "right" background. No, it is used by a variety of people from all walks of life who know the power visualization has on the *positive* outcomes of their dreams, goals, and desires.[88]

There are countless stories of athletes who visualize themselves breaking a record, making the touchdown, kicking the winning field goal, scoring the final points for the game, or belting out a home run when they get to the plate. The actors who visualize themselves changing into character on stage or in film become so believably transformed that they give an award-winning performance. These are the individuals who use visualization to achieve the exact positive outcome of whatever their intention, desire, or goal.

Visualization is so powerful that it is always part of my life, not just during my retreats but virtually every day. I use visualization to "see" the outcomes of every task, project, or goal I am working toward. I follow six steps to visualize and manifest the life I want to live, and these are easily mastered by anyone who wishes for regular success.

1. *Have a definite idea of what you want*— In order to attain exactly what you want, it is vital to have a precise and clear image of what you want and why you want it. Just saying you want to be rich won't make it so. You have to have a clear idea of what you will do

professionally to attain the wealth you desire. I would argue that you need to think in terms of accomplishments and success rather than just getting money, which is a byproduct of your achievements.

First, you must have a clear understanding of what it will bring to your life and your happiness. Sometimes, what you want is only a steppingstone to something even greater that will be transformative to your entire life. Life is a process, and you will often take numerous steps to reach your ultimate goals.

Look at Oprah Winfrey; she started out as a newscaster who transitioned from a news anchor to a talk show host, and then she built a media empire. As far as I can tell, she continues to grow and expand her various businesses and, in doing so, touches countless lives worldwide. She uses and swears by visualization. Not everyone will be an Oprah, but that's okay; just don't hold back on what you want. Think about exactly what you want your life to be—what is that big idea or idea that will get you to that point?

2. *Stillness and meditation*—This step is easily accomplished when you are on your retreat in your happy place, but it can be done daily and anywhere with a little effort. Sitting in stillness and focusing on your breathing to get into a meditative state only requires a place where you can be undisturbed for a specific amount of time that you determine. I recommend thirty minutes. That is enough time to bring yourself into a controlled state of calmness. During your normal daily routine, this could be early in the morning, before work,

or late at night, after you have gotten home and finished dinner, put the kids to bed, etc. This can be done in a home office, a walk-in closet, the she-shed, or anywhere you can carve out fifteen to thirty minutes of time with no interruptions to bring your breathing down to a slow, steady pace while you begin to visualize your goal.

3. *Think about your goal and visualize it in absolute detail*—This is where you can use your imagination to vividly create a clear picture of the result of your intentions or goals. Make this as complete a vision as possible with even the most minute detail you can imagine. You can write all its details in your journal, conjure up the vision in your mind daily, or even create a vision board complete with pictures of everything associated with achieving your goal.

A vision board can help with visualization and consists of just cutting out pictures of things that inspire you toward your goals. It is a matter of going through magazines, cutting out pictures, and pasting them down on a piece of cardboard or foam core (or, of course, digitally on Pinterest). If you desire to have a beach house, for example, then your vision board might consist of a series of pictures of beach houses you are particularly fond of, along with beach views, boats, sunsets, and anything that makes you happy and is related to your goal. Think of it as your roadmap to a destination.

4. *Create the feelings of achieving your visualized goal*—When you start to visualize the actual outcome of what you want in life, it is

important not only to visualize but also to actually "feel" exactly what it will be like to achieve your desire or goal. What will it look like to get what you want? How will you feel emotionally to get what you want? What will it smell like to be in the place where you get what you want? What will it sound like? Involve all your senses in this visualization of getting what you want when it happens. Imagine what it will be like when you attain your goal, how it will feel, what you will see, what sounds you will hear, and what you will smell.

In the beach house example, it means to feel what it would be like to have the sand pressing between your toes as you walk along the beach in front of your house, smell the salt air while you listen to the breeze rustling the tall grass in the dunes off the deck of your home, and taste the tropical cocktail you're sipping as you look out at the views. Think in terms of every aspect of what it will be like and how it will feel to reach that desired goal.

5. *Spend time daily taking action to achieve your goal*—Don't view getting what you want as a race you have to rush to finish. Instead, look at it as a process that can take years to achieve. It is a journey. I have talked about breaking down your goals into small chunks to make the process more manageable and less daunting. I ask myself daily what I can accomplish today to chip away at reaching my overall goal. Any task, no matter how complex, can be broken down into a series of very doable and achievable steps that will take me methodically along the path until the end result is reached.

It is discouraging to focus on how far out the end goal is because that could result in quitting before you achieve it. But, if I focus on the individual steps I achieve daily, weekly, and monthly, I will have more frequent and immediate satisfaction in knowing that I have completed each step, or mini-goal, to reach the actual larger goal completion. Every journey begins with that first step.

6. *Never give up*— One of the most important aspects of visualization is following through with the repetitive visualizing of your goals. You must continuously visualize your goal until it becomes engrained in your psyche. This is where many people fail because they quit on the follow-through or think it is a waste of time because nothing has happened immediately. Winston Churchill said in a speech, "Never give up on something that you can't go a day without thinking about."

If you believe in your goal, truly believe and visualize that you will achieve it, and think about it every day—on your personal retreats and in your daily life. You have to stick with the belief in your goal until you reach it, regardless of any failures or setbacks along the way. Thinking about and visualizing it for one day and then forgetting about it means you have abandoned your goal. Astronaut Sally Ride, the first American woman in space, famously said, "You can't be what you can't see." You have to live and breathe your goals every day, every week, every month, and every year until you attain the desired result you have visualized.

Countless people don't have the wherewithal to follow through on reaching their goals. Have you ever heard a friend or colleague make a New Year's resolution to lose weight or start exercising? They have good intentions but ultimately give up on it a week or two or a month later. I see this every new year. Why do you think the weight loss programs and gyms advertise heavily every January?

I believe that if you never give up and never quit reaching for your goals, you will eventually attain them. The "never give up" step is likely the hardest and requires dedication and a will to work fiercely. By recognizing that it is hard, you can mentally prepare yourself for it and take the necessary steps that I've outlined here to increase your chances of success.

Quick Tips:

1. Think about your goal and visualize it in absolute detail.
2. When you start to visualize the actual outcome of what you want in life, it is important not only to visualize but also to "feel" exactly what it will be like to achieve your desire or goal.
3. Spend time daily taking actions to achieve your goal.
4. Never give up. One of the most important aspects of visualization is following through with the repetitive visualizing of your goals. You must continuously visualize your goal until it becomes engrained in your psyche.

Worksheet:

Using Visualization on a Personal Retreat

Part 1: Setting the Stage

1. Identify the specific goal or challenge you want to focus on during your personal retreat.

   _____

   _____

   _____

2. Determine how visualization can support your goal or challenge.

   _____

   _____

   _____

   _____

3. Create an environment that supports visualization, such as a quiet space with minimal distractions.

   _____

   _____

   _____

Part 2: Practicing Visualization Exercises

1. Engage in visualization exercises that support your goal or challenge, such as guided imagery or mental rehearsal.

   _____

   _____

   _____

2. Use all of your senses to make your visualization experience as vivid and realistic as possible.

   _____

3. Practice visualization exercises regularly throughout your retreat.

   _____

Part 3: Reflecting on Your Visualization

1. Reflect on your visualization experience and the insights or ideas you have generated.

   _____

   _____

   _____

_____

_____

_____

2. Use your reflections to refine your visualizations and identify any potential roadblocks or challenges.

_____

_____

_____

_____

_____

3. Determine any action steps needed to implement your ideas and achieve your goal.

_____

_____

_____

_____

_____

Part 4: Expanding Your Visualization

1. Challenge yourself to visualize beyond your current patterns and assumptions.

   _____

   _____

2. Engage in activities that stimulate your imagination and creativity, such as reading or exploring new environments.

   _____

   _____

3. Practice visualization exercises in different settings or environments to expand your visualizations.

   _____

   _____

Part 5: Implementing Your Visualizations

1. Create an action plan for implementing your visualizations.

   _____

   _____

_____

_____

_____

_____

_____

_____

2. Identify any support or resources you may need, such as a vision board to aid in your visualizations.

_____

_____

_____

3. Set a timeline for completing the visualization of each action step and hold yourself accountable.

_____

_____

_____

_____

_____

_____

Part 6: Reflection

1. After your personal retreat, reflect on your overall experience and the insights or ideas you generated through visualization.

_____

_____

_____

_____

_____

_____

_____

_____

2. Consider any insights or lessons you gained during your retreat that can help you continue to use visualization in your daily life.

_____

_____

_____

_____

_____

_____

_____

_____

_____

3. Use your reflections to create a plan for implementing your visualizations and continuing to expand your visualization practice.

_____

_____

_____

_____

_____

_____

_____

_____

_____

_____

_____

_____

_____

_____

— ◯ —

Remember, visualization is a powerful tool for personal growth and development. Use this worksheet to help you set the stage for visualization, practice visualization exercises, reflect on your experience, expand your visualization practice, implement your visualizations, and reflect on your overall experience.

— What to Expect on the Retreat —

When I go on my annual personal retreat, I fly from Los Angeles to Boston. After arrival, I get a rental car, and it is another four and half hour's drive up into the northern reaches of coastal Maine. I have a definite plan for the road trip portion—several hours into the drive, I stop at a big box store to pick up the items I chose not to bring in my luggage, like toothpaste, mouthwash, water, trail mix, etc. Then, it's usually another two-hour or so drive to my final destination.

Once there, I settle into my accommodations by completely unpacking, which doesn't take long because I pack smartly. I hang up all my clothes, put my reading material on the dresser, my journal on the nightstand, and my empty suitcase in the corner of the room, out of the way. I want to make myself feel right at home and not like I'm living out of a suitcase. To me, a complete unpacking is an important step because it makes me feel like I will be there for a while, and I can start to slow down. Even though it is a week or so, constantly digging things out of a suitcase makes me think about when I will be leaving. I want to be in the moment each day and not think about my departure until I absolutely have to, which is the night before I leave.

At this point, unpacked, I begin the process of winding down from my normal everyday life. There are several things I tend to do immediately. I sit and reread my intentions for the retreat, goals, and anything else I have written in my journal in the weeks and months leading up to my alone time. This is when I start to focus on these written items, and I will continue to reference them each day of the retreat. I will begin each morning by reviewing that material so it is fresh in my mind. This allows me to see what will bubble to the surface of my mind on that particular day.

Reading my intentions and goals each day is like flipping through a magazine. I will stop on one item that strikes a chord in me that day and start to contemplate that one thing. I may review my intentions, goals, and other writings while sitting in my room or while I am having breakfast. It doesn't matter to me where you do it, as long as it is at the beginning of the day. The clarity of the morning is helpful in staying focused on the purpose of the retreat, and I carry my journal with me throughout the day not just to reference but also to add more thoughts, ideas, and notes.

When I have finished breakfast, I go outside, sit on the porch of the boardinghouse, and soak in the morning by continuing my thinking process, which I started while reviewing my journal notes. The weather will dictate what I'm going to do next. If the sun is shining, I go somewhere other than where I'm staying. On the other hand, if it is raining, I'll likely go into the living room and read or journal for the morning. This is why I have a loose schedule— to allow for the day to unfold in a more organic fashion. Doing so contributes to the reduction of stress and just makes for a much more relaxed day in which I will still get a lot accomplished in my mind.

When it's beautiful out, I head to a secluded local spot where I can set up my camp chair and be completely alone. I *only* bring my chair, journal, some reading material, and a bottle of water. It is important to stay hydrated, and plain water is all I need. The spot I identified decades ago has not changed in the ensuing years that I have been sitting there for a week or more each summer. I may sit there for three or four hours during the morning thinking, reading, thinking some more, and maybe even napping. The thing about napping is that your subconscious mind is still working away while you are sleeping. If you were focused on a problem or new idea just before dozing off, your subconscious is working on it as you sleep.

Your subconscious mind is always working as it controls all your involuntary bodily functions like your heartbeat, digestion, breathing, blood circulation, and more. Inventor Thomas Edison said, "Never go to sleep without a request to your subconscious." He meant that before you go to sleep, you can think about or write down a goal or ask yourself questions about a problem you are trying to solve. Spend five or ten minutes thinking about the goal or the questions intently. The more specific you are, the better. While sleeping, your subconscious mind will work on solutions and answers for you.[89]

I have awakened from a nap on these annual retreats only to have had an epiphany or clarity on whatever it was that I was thinking about. It never ceases to amaze me how much lucidity deep thought will bring to an intention, goal, or other topic, regardless of how small or grand it may be in the scheme of your world. So, whether you are napping or awake during these blocks of time sitting alone, your mind is still engaged consciously or subconsciously.

During those periods, I use my full imagination and visualization skills in conjunction with deep thought and mindfulness. That is when the real magic begins. The hours of sitting are where the real work of the personal retreat happens, and my mind will be firing on all cylinders. I love sitting in the sun overlooking the cove. The sun is warm but usually not too hot, and it is kept in check by the light breeze coming off the ocean beyond. There is a serenity to sitting there immersed in nature and a sense of being in a safe, calm place—a place where I can strip away any protective facade that is ever present in my regular life.

At about noon, I start to feel a little hungry and go to pick up the sandwich I ordered for lunch earlier that morning. I may drive or walk depending on how I feel. Sometimes, after an intense emotional morning, I may opt for additional exercise by walking to pick up my lunch and walking back to a nearby old weathered picnic table.

I will eat lunch while looking out at the water, continuing to be in my thoughts, alone, enjoying the blissful mid-day sun and ocean breeze. I try to take a full hour for lunch and may even go for another walk after eating. I sometimes like to take a very leisurely stroll along the shoreline, stopping to look at driftwood, seagrass, shells, or whatever else may have washed up on the beach during high tide. It's not a strenuous walk, but it is different, and I don't get to do that any other time of year except when I'm on the retreat. These natural objects along the shore keep my mind active, inspiring me to look at things differently.

If it is a particularly gorgeous day, I may decide to go for a drive into the nearby town to get a soft-serve ice cream cone. A twenty-minute drive takes me through a rural wooded area, and the road sometimes hugs the coastline, revealing spectacular views of a bay dotted with sailboats and lobster boats. I travel over two small bridges connecting a tiny island to the mainland. The second bridge has a lovely view of another sheltered cove home to a half-dozen boats and the most beautiful red boathouse on a granite ledge. At low tide, you can see the metal rails the boat cradle travels along when the owners pull their boats out for the season.

The town is a scenic little Maine village on the water with a handful of restaurants, galleries, and a hardware store. The place feels active but not overwhelmingly busy as I make my way to a small family-run roadside eatery. It is known for its lobster rolls and fried whole-belly clams, but they also have soft-serve ice cream, and I get a vanilla cone. There really is nothing like a cold ice cream cone on a warm summer day. I may sit and eat the cone at an outside table or get back in my car and continue to drive. It is all based on how I feel and what I fancy at the moment. That is one of the keys to the personal retreat—carefreeness. You do what you want as long as you can be alone and think.

After finishing my cone, I will likely go back to that secluded spot where I spent my morning and sit there again in the afternoon. If I have spent four hours or so in the morning in deep thought, I may only spend a few hours doing that in the afternoon. My experience has been that four or five hours in a state of mindfulness is about all I will do in a day. That doesn't mean I am not continuing to think about my intentions and goals during waking hours. It means I am not doing it intently in a state of mindfulness.

On some afternoons, I explore the area. I may go to a little museum or go for a sail. There may be some fair or arts festival going on somewhere in the region I can drive to. I do this alone and in my own world, always thinking about my intentions and goals during this period.

By late afternoon, I will make my way back to the boarding house and get washed up for dinner. I may sit and read a book for a little while before eating or maybe journal. It is all about how I feel and what I want to do, free from external influences. After dinner, I may continue to read, go for another walk, or drive to a special spot to watch the sunset over a local harbor. I will usually watch the sunset if there are enough clouds in the sky. The most picturesque sunsets happen when there are a fair amount of clouds for the sunlight to illuminate with a rainbow of colors. Just the act of watching a sunset alone and marveling at the glory of nature adds to the stillness of the retreat.

How often do any of us stop and watch a sunrise or sunset? It usually isn't nearly often enough, and doing it on your retreat will remind you that it is important in life to slow down, absorb the natural world around you, and stop and smell the flowers periodically. We must reflect on our lives and distill out what is truly important. During these times, I can get the greatest clarity and focus that I can fully utilize in the months and year ahead. It is about understanding my own purpose and what I can contribute to the world and the greater humanity. This is something that you will find bubbling up in your thoughts.

By 9:00 PM, I am in bed, ready to let my subconscious mind work on what I focused on during the day and to get a very restful night's sleep. I will repeat the same routine, with some variations, each day of my retreat. If I travel to my destination on a Saturday, my retreat usually starts on a Sunday morning and will run through the following Friday. If I am taking a class, my retreat will begin the day after I complete the course. Either way, I will have at least six to seven days allocated for my personal retreat. Whatever time you take for your personal retreat is best for you; it is your choice. Remember, the entire concept of a personal retreat is based on the choices you make regarding when you take it, for how long, and where you will find your happy place.

This is what my typical daily routine is each day for my entire personal retreat week. As you can see, it is not overly scheduled with all kinds of organized activities. There are no group events, yoga classes, or sing-a-longs around a campfire. None of that is needed if you are serious about taking the necessary alone time for yourself. All you really need is yourself, a journal, some reading material relevant to your intentions and goals, and a secluded place to sit. If you have that, you are on your way to discovering what you need to achieve your goals and desires and make profound changes in your life.

When my retreat is over and I head home— aside from being relaxed, refreshed, and recharged—I am very motivated to follow through on the results of my retreat. I will review my journal on the flight home and continue to reference and write in my journal daily. The follow-through on your intentions and goals is as important as the retreat itself. If you don't follow through on your plans to achieve your goals, then the retreat was nothing more than a vacation that quickly fades into your memory. If you took the time to take a personal retreat and followed the ideas I have presented, you should be able to continue the momentum you established during your time alone.

I am very motivated when I return from my retreats and dive right into measuring the progress toward my goals on a daily and weekly basis. Coming home from my retreat, I have at least one or two major goals I will focus on accomplishing in the year ahead. There are also small goals and intentions that I continue to review and work on in a logical order that are usually related to or are part of the major goals. It is a constant process of reviewing my journal, measuring my progress, and then crossing off the goal when achieved so I can move on to the next goal.

It sounds easy enough, but it is difficult for those who are insecure about being alone for any length of time. Clinical psychologists have encountered many patients over the years who have a genuine discomfort or outright fear of being alone.[90] The connected world we live in today is often used as a surrogate to combat being alone by being online, texting or messaging, chatting on the phone, or always having the television on as a "companion." Some experience FOMO, the fear of missing out, if they are alone without any contact with their friends or peers. Now, some of this may be a serious psychological condition that requires psychotherapy. Still, barring that, it is just a bad habit we all have gotten into for the simple fear of being alone or missing out on something.

Put the devices away, and don't worry about what others are doing. The social media likes don't matter, and missing a get-together with friends isn't that important in the bigger scheme of things. Only you can decide what is truly important to you. No one else can or should make those choices for you, and no one should ever set goals for you. You, and only you, can and should develop the capacity to be alone *well*, in a positive frame of mind. One psychologist describes being alone well as "developing a greater tolerance for, and intimacy with, your experience — the emotional, cognitive, visceral, imaginative, and sensory moment-to-moment arisings that constitute your basic aliveness."[91] This is what being alone is all about on your retreat: being more in touch with yourself, your aliveness, and what you want from life. Being alone for a day or a week should not be feared but rather embraced for the positive experience of improving your life.

What matters most is that you are concerned with *you* and *you* alone on your personal retreat. This is your time to reflect and ruminate on the various aspects of your life, how you live, and what you want to do with it for your remaining time. It is your time to seek out what you want most: the answers to your burning desires and how to achieve your goals. Those answers are inside of you if you are willing to take the time and steps to discover them, which is what the *Find Your Happy Place* personal retreat is all about. It is about intimate personal discovery through the process of deep thought—your ability to imagine and visualize your life and desires for the future.

I cannot emphasize this enough: you have to spend quality time alone if you are going to set goals and make a plan to achieve those goals. Once you reach a goal, set another and another. It is a never-ending process. Embrace the time alone, whether an afternoon, a day, a week, or more. It is your time—*me time*—make the most of it.

Don't be afraid to take more than one retreat a year, especially if you can only do a half or full day initially. It is okay to build into a long personal retreat, like dipping your toe in the water. As you become more acclimated to the notion of being alone to think about your goals and future, it will be easier to expand the amount of time you allocate to your retreat. Remember it is not about how far away from your regular environment you go, just so long as you get some distance. That can be across town, the other side of the state, or across the country as long as you change up your daily routines and space. Understanding the purpose of your retreat and the mindset you want to be in when you take this special time alone is crucial to the success of your retreat. This is your time, and you should utilize it in the most efficient ways possible. You can do a retreat for little or no budget, so there are no excuses for not trying this out for at least a day.

I often take a "mini-retreat" throughout the year. I may bring something to read or not, but I am alone and in my own headspace. It is easy enough to do these mini-retreats if you set your mind to it. Realize how much time you waste doing mindless things like watching television or making excuses for not having time to spend on your own. Just take a moment and look at your week; I'll bet you can find plenty of time to indulge in a mini-retreat, especially on a weekend or your day off.

It is also important for you not to feel at all guilty, in any way, about taking this time for yourself. Not only do you need to do this annually, but you should encourage your loved ones to do the same. Each of us must take some time for ourselves and reflect on our own setbacks, successes, and what we want out of life in the coming year. It should be an annual event that is looked forward to and cherished as a special part of your yearly life, just like a birthday.

As I have mentioned, my wife is fully supportive of me taking my annual retreat to Maine. I am equally supportive of her taking the time she needs each year for herself. In fact, when I am gone for my retreat, she also has time to do whatever she wants. We both feel it has strengthened our relationship and made us more centered individuals and a happier couple.

Sometimes, people think of a retreat as something you take when life is hard or things are rough, and you need to get away from it all to regroup. That is not the case with *Find Your Happy Place.* Sure, there will be times when life has thrown you a curve ball, and you will need more than ever to reflect on it so that you can map out a game plan to course correct. But the hope is that most of the time, you are doing well. The personal retreat is your time to reflect on your accomplishments and continue building on those successes in the coming year. By doing this consistently on an annual basis, you will find that there is more consistency in your achievements and a continual follow-through on your intentions and goals. In turn, you will feel better and have a more positive attitude about your life path.

Once you start to take your personal retreat annually, it is okay to make adjustments and revisions from year to year. After you have done your first one, you will find out quickly exactly what worked and what didn't. Maybe the locale wasn't right, or you took too much or too little time. These are all things learned through trial and error that you can tweak for the next retreat you take.

Even though I have been going on my annual retreat for decades, I continue to make small adjustments and try new things. Some work, some don't, but at least I have tried them out, and my next retreat will be slightly different because it is always good to keep experimenting and changing things up a little.

Quick Tips:

1. Make this the year you take your personal retreat and boost your creative thinking.
2. Determine the right amount of time and when best to take that time during the year for your personal retreat.
3. Make sure that your happy place is free from diversions and interruptions so that you can achieve deep thought. It's okay to try different locations over several retreats. It is about finding the perfect spot for you that will allow you to maximize the benefits of your personal retreat.
4. If you don't already, start journaling as soon as you are in the planning stages of your personal retreat. Writing longhand in your journal has a cognitive effect and will pay dividends in keeping your mind sharp. It taps into the creative side of your brain to bring out imaginative solutions to the issues and topics you are thinking and writing about.
5. The location of your retreat will dictate what you will need to bring for clothing and footwear.
6. Having a healthy mind, active imagination, and a healthy body

means taking care of yourself with exercise and nutrition. The simple act of walking is proven to be good cardio exercise. Walking lowers your stress level and gives you more energy while building stamina.

7. Deciding on and setting achievable goals boils down to understanding what goals are and how they are reached. Wishes are nothing more than goals not followed through on. Progress toward your goals comes more quickly when you focus on one goal at a time.

8. Stillness is not about being completely motionless but being in the moment alone in a place with little or no distractions. There is nothing to be terrified of by being alone for a period of time. Being alone is for the specific motivation of self-reflection and self-improvement. It is about scheduling alone time or *me time* for yourself in relation to your personal retreat.

9. Research has shown that some of the most creative thinkers in history also spent a lot of quality time working at their craft or profession alone. *Find Your Happy Place* for a personal retreat will ignite your imagination and boost your creativity.

— The Journey to Find Your Happy Place —

As I mentioned at the beginning of this book, my annual personal retreat saved me during a period of loss and trauma in my life. Frankly, I don't know if I would have survived the way I did if it was not for my own personal retreat. It was a lifeline that tethered me from going under physically and emotionally. Traveling to Maine alone, sitting in deep thought about what was going on in my life, and formulating a game plan for the coming year was the prescription I needed. It allowed me to determine the next steps to change my trajectory.

When I reflect on that period of time, I have the perspective to realize how lucky I was to have taken my personal retreats. It gave me the time needed to formulate my goals and the plan to achieve them, which I did. The retreat offered me the tools to improve my situation.

Everything I have written in this book is based on my experiences over decades. It is tried, true, and tested by me year in and year out. It's a roadmap I am passing on to you so that you can experience the same successes I have achieved over the years. But realize that it requires a lot of hard work. You will have to make changes, sacrifices, and course-correct your life path if you want to reach your most fervent goals.

Today, there seems to be resistance to hard work for some.

Many want to opt for a shortcut— the easy way. We have become a society of instant gratification where everything is immediate— same-day delivery, next-day delivery, the proliferation of delivery services, ridesharing, and apps that do nearly everything with instant results. If you truly want to make changes in where you are and what you are doing with your life, it will require hard work. There is no shortcut. But once you have dedicated yourself to going on a personal retreat, deep thinking, setting goals, and making an achievable plan, I guarantee you will do it.

My journey is proof that once you commit yourself to *Find Your Happy Place*, you will be amazed at how far you can soar. I thought working for a company for almost thirty-three years meant I was on a treadmill—a gerbil wheel—with no way off. That I was destined to continue in those miserable circumstances for years to come. I would have if I didn't have the wherewithal to make a change. I was already conditioned from years of taking my annual retreat. I thought long and hard about my situation and how I could change it. That allowed me to come up with a detailed plan—a road map to improve my circumstances.

After I set the ball in motion on my plan, I took two years to exit the company on my own terms. With the help of an employment attorney, I was able to leave well set up to pursue my passion of writing full-time, which was one of my goals. The company also gave me my coveted vintage Kem Weber-designed Disney animation desk, along with other perks. That desk ultimately inspired me to write a book on the midcentury modern animation desks and related furniture. That was a happy byproduct of my plan—an opportunity that presented itself and one that I seized.

It was still a bittersweet departure. I loved the company and what it stood for but decided that I could better enjoy the good parts of it on the outside through my writing. That has been the most satisfying as I have researched and written on the topics I chose. It gives me the freedom to tell the stories I want to tell without the stress of the daily grind of reporting to and dealing with individuals who do not appreciate me or my contributions.

More than seven years since leaving, as of this book release, I am still writing full-time and have never been more relaxed in my life. I am eating well and exercising daily. A number of people have told me that I look much younger than my age, which is proof that the toxic stress has dissipated.

My outlook is ever positive as I plan more projects and books out into the future. I continue taking my annual retreat and mini retreats throughout the year. On each retreat, I reflect on the previous year's accomplishments, set new goals for the year ahead, and further add to the list of books I want to write. *Find Your Happy Place* has turned into a way of life that keeps on giving with abundance. I am living proof of that!

I could not have gone through the last thirty-plus years without a plan and the optimistic view that I *can* change my circumstances. My life plans—or maps, if you will— have come out of the *Find Your Happy Place* retreats. I hope you will also experience significant success through the plan and experiences I have shared with you throughout this book. It is up to you to go beyond just reading this book and implement the steps I have passionately laid out for you.

Theodore Roosevelt once said, "Believe you can, and you're halfway there." That is a very true statement. It is all within yourself—the belief that you can and will accomplish your goals. That is the real secret to success: believing in yourself. Only you can be laser-focused on where you want to go in life and what you want to accomplish.

Like any journey, it starts with a first step. You will also need a map, and your goals are the destinations along your journey. Without a map, you will be lost. Your journey will be an aimless meandering with no sense of direction. It is impossible to know where you are going without a plan, and therefore, you will never arrive at a final goal. I say this so that you will pause for a moment and think about your own situation. Where are you, and where do you want to go? If you are like many, you might just say, "I don't know." That is why you need a plan—a map to follow.

No one will give you that map or plan. It is within you to come up with it and to build on it. And I want you to know this: no one will believe in you until you believe in yourself. Let me say that again: no one will believe in *you* until *you believe in yourself*!

You must take that first step. You have to put the negative

voices out of your head and start the ball in motion to change your situation. No one is going to come up to you and say, "Hey, your life is going nowhere. Let me get you on the right track to the life you should be leading." That will not happen. What does happen every day is that individuals, just like you, make a choice to change their situation to go after their dreams and the life they want.

Zig Ziglar was a renowned motivational speaker and author who inspired millions of people around the world with his powerful messages on personal growth and success. One of his most famous teachings was on the importance of setting goals for success. Ziglar believed that setting clear and specific goals is crucial for success in any area of life, whether personal, professional, or financial. He emphasized the need for individuals to have a strong sense of purpose and direction and to continually review and adjust their goals to stay on track and achieve their desired outcomes.[92]

Ziglar once said, "When you discipline yourself to do those things you ought to do when you ought to do them, the day will come when you can do the things you want to do when you want to do them."[93] You must reach for that discipline, that strength from within, to take charge of your life and stop letting others tell you what you should or shouldn't be doing. You, and you alone, are the only person who can do it. When you realize the power of goal setting and that the discipline to work toward those goals comes from within, you will take charge to create the life you want. Just stop drifting through life without a rudder and find the compass within you to follow your dreams.

Embarking on a personal retreat is an extraordinary endeavor that holds the power to ignite profound transformation within you. It is a sacred opportunity to recharge, reflect, and reconnect with your truest self. As you delve into the depths of this journey, remember the significance of following through on your intentions. It is not enough to simply gain insights and set goals during your retreat; you must create an action plan to bring those intentions to life.

Visualize a future where your dreams and aspirations become your reality. It begins by compiling a list of actionable steps to guide you on your post-retreat path. Take the time to set a timeline for achieving these goals, injecting them with purpose and urgency. And don't underestimate the power of accountability—reach out to friends, family, or a mentor who can offer support and hold you to your intentions. Surround yourself with individuals who believe in your potential and are committed to seeing you succeed.

Remember, this personal retreat you embark upon has the power to shape your destiny. It is a transformative experience that transcends the boundaries of time and space, nurturing your imagination and expanding your creativity. The principles I have shared—seclusion, goal setting, stillness, deep thought or mindfulness, imagination, journaling, and being present—are your steadfast companions on this remarkable journey of self-discovery and self-improvement. They serve as the compass guiding you toward a life that aligns with your deepest desires.

Now, it is time to seize the moment and embark on your personal retreat. Embrace the life-changing benefits that await you as you tap into the boundless reservoirs of your creativity. Let your retreat be the catalyst that propels you toward the life you yearn for and deserve. Take this opportunity to redefine your purpose, amplify your passions, and manifest your dreams. Believe in yourself and the power within you to effect profound change. Embrace this journey with unwavering determination and embrace the extraordinary transformation that awaits you as you *Find Your Happy Place.* The time is now. Go forth and lead the life you deserve and have always desired.

— Epilogue —

Throughout the pages of this book, I have consistently emphasized the significance of discovering one's own happy place, an essential milestone I reached over three decades ago. These retreats have been the foundation of my journey—a blueprint that propelled me toward greater heights of happiness and accomplishment. However, in this chaotic world, the power to instigate the necessary changes for attaining our desired happiness and success resides entirely within us. I convey this message with utmost sincerity because the countless self-help books available hold no value unless we take action. The genuine secret to altering the course of our lives and realizing our dreams lies within us; it always has. We are surrounded by thousands of stories of individuals who, against all odds, emerged from poverty, failure, or dire circumstances to achieve remarkable success and happiness. These stories, both inspiring and motivating, serve as a testament to what can be accomplished if we believe in ourselves. Remember, before others believe in us, we must first believe in ourselves. Regardless of our current circumstances, we possess the capacity to change and live the life we desire.

Find Your Happy Place: The 8-Step Guide to Boosting Your Creativity Through a Personal Retreat has been an invaluable asset to me, and it can be the same for you. It is not a magical elixir reserved for a select few; rather, it is a roadmap you can adapt and customize to suit your needs. If you genuinely believe in yourself, maintain an unwavering focus on your goals, and persevere, you will witness the fruits of your labor. This process may take years; no one ever claimed it would be effortless. Ultimately, the outcome you derive from the methods elucidated in this book is directly proportional to the effort you invest.

It is my hope that you will revisit sections of this book, jot down personal notes in the margins, and continue to journal and diligently pursue your goals. This is a continuous process that requires daily, weekly, monthly, and yearly reviews and revisions. If you adhere to this practice, I assure you that you will experience tangible results. The successive triumphs you encounter will not be a matter of luck but rather the direct consequence of your tireless work and unwavering commitment.

In conclusion, the power to shape your own destiny lies within your hands. By embracing the principles outlined in this book and by persistently striving toward your goals, you will embark on a transformative journey. It works for me, and there is no reason it can't work for you if you put in the essential effort. Let us remember that true fulfillment and accomplishment arise not from external factors but from our own resilience, dedication, and self-belief. May your pursuit of happiness and success be an unwavering testament to the indomitable spirit that resides within you.

— About the Author —

David A. Bossert is an accomplished artist, filmmaker, and author with 40+ years of experience in the animation industry. He spent more than thirty-two years at Walt Disney Animation Studios, where he contributed his talents to films such as *The Black Cauldron* (1985) *Who Framed Roger Rabbit* (1988), *The Little Mermaid* (1989), *Beauty and the Beast* (1991), *Aladdin* (1992), *Tim Burton's The Nightmare Before Christmas* (1993), *The Lion King* (1994), *Fantasia/2000* (1999), and Destino (2003) among many others. Throughout his career, Bossert has been recognized for his creative and innovative contributions to the field, including earning several United States patents for his work on digital imaging.

Bossert is a member of the CalArts Board of Trustees, Visual Effects Society (VES), Academy of Motion Picture Arts and Sciences (AMPAS) and has been a visiting scholar at Carnegie Mellon University's Entertainment Technology Center (ETC) in Pittsburgh. He has presented and lectured at the Museum of Fine Arts Boston, Los Angeles County Museum of Art, The Salvador Dali Museum, School of Visual Arts, NYU Film School, Bowers Museum, Newport Beach Film Festival, Fundació Gala-Salvador Dalí (Figueres, Spain), Oscar Pomillio-Blumm Forum (Pescara, Italy), and at other venues and festivals. Bossert, a historian, is widely regarded as an expert in the realm of Disney animation art, process, and history.

In addition to his achievements in animation, Bossert has also established himself as a prolific award-winning writer, boasting numerous published articles and more than a dozen books to his name. His literary works encompass a variety of subjects, including animation and theme park history, design, and the creative process. Bossert attributes much of his success to his annual retreats spanning more than thirty years, which serve as the foundation for his book, *"Find Your Happy Place: The 8-Step Guide to Boosting Your Creativity through a Personal Retreat."* Further information can be found at www.davidbossert.com.

— Other Books —

BY DAVID A. BOSSERT

Remembering Roy E. Disney: *Memories and Photos of a Storied Life*

—

Dali and Disney: Destino—
The Story, Artwork, and Friendship Behind the Legendary Film

—

An Animator's Gallery: *Eric Goldberg Draws the Disney Characters*

—

Oswald The Lucky Rabbit: *The Search for The Lost Disney Cartoons*

—

Kem Weber: *Mid-Century Furniture Designs for the Disney Studios*

—

Oswald The Lucky Rabbit:
The Search for The Lost Disney Cartoons SPECIAL EDITION

—

The Art of Tennessee Loveless:
10 X 10 X 10 - The Mickey Mouse Contemporary Pop Art Series

—

3D Disneyland: *Like You've Never Seen It Before*

—

The Art of George Scribner: *The Panama Canal Painting*

—

Claude Coats: *Walt Disney's Imagineer, The Making of Disneyland*

—

3D National Parks: *Like You've Never Seen Them Before*

—

Tim Burton's The Nightmare Before Christmas Visual Companion

—

The House of the Future:
Walt Disney, MIT, and Monsanto's Vision of Tomorrow

— Endnotes —

1   *21 Zig Ziglar Quotes to Inspire Your Success in Life and Business*, by Peter Economy, Inc.com, Oct 2, 2015

2   *On this day 22 years ago, Bill Gates wrote his legendary "Internet Tidal Wave" memo*, by Harry McCracken, May 26, 2017, Fast Company; https://www.fastcompany.com/4039009/22-years-ago-today-bill-gates-wrote-his-legendary-internet-tidal-wave-memo

3   Bill Gates Spends Two Weeks Alone In The Forest Each Year. Here's Why; Thriveglobal.com; July 23, 2018

4   Bill Gates Spends Two Weeks Alone In The Forest Each Year. Here's Why; Thriveglobal.com; July 23, 2018

5   *Sleep Deprivation and Deficiency*, NIH, National Heart, Lung and Blood Institute; U.S. Department of Health & Human Services, https://www.nhlbi.nih.gov/health-topics/sleep-deprivation-and-deficiency

6   CDC resource: https://www.cdc.gov/diabetes/library/features/diabetes-sleep.html

7   *Oxford English Dictionary*, Oxford University Press, 2019

8   Effects of Mindfulness on Psychological Health: A Review of Empirical Studies, NIH National Library of Medicine, Shian-Ling Keng, Moria J. Smoski, and Clive J. Robinsa,, Jun 11, 2013

9   *"A translational neuroscience perspective on mindfulness meditation as a prevention strategy", by Tang, Yi-Yuan; Leve, Leslie D. (2015); Translational Behavioral Medicine. 6 (1): 63–72.*

10   The Most Luxe Vacation Is Unplugged, by Ellen Ganerman; Pg. A11, The Wall Street Journal, June 30, 2019

11   Downeast Photography Workshops; https://shop.downeast.com/photography-workshops/

12   Ann Arbor Art Center, https://www.annarborartcenter.org/education/upcoming-classes/

13   American Academy of Bookbinding, https://www.bookbindingacademy.org/courses/

14   The Iowa Summer Writing Festival, https://iowasummerwritingfestival.org/workshop

15   Woodenboat School, https://www.thewoodenboatschool.com/index.php

16   Pacific Northwest Sculptors, http://www.pnwsculptors.org/classes.htm

17   Woodworking School Directory, Fine Woodworking, https://www.finewoodworking.com/2007/01/18/woodworking-schools-directory

18   Woodley Park Archers, Los Angeles, California; http://woodleyparkarchers.org/

19   American Sailing Association; https://asa.com/learn-to-sail/

20   Calvert Quilt Shop, Maryland; http://www.calvertquiltshop.com/classes.htm

21   Build a Kayak, The Center for Wooden Boats, Seattle, WA; https://www.cwb.org/kayak

22   Basketry classes, The North House Folk School, https://northhouse.org/courses/category/basketry

23   Armory Art Center, West Palm Beach, Florida; https://www.armoryart.org/printmaking

24   Haystack Mountain School of Crafts, Deer Isle, Maine; https://www.haystack-mtn.org/about-haystack/

25   The Center for Furniture Craftsmanship, Rockport, Maine; https://www.woodschool.org/about-wood-school-maine/general-information-wood-school

26   Iyer, Pico, *The Art of Stillness*, TED Books, 2014; pg.42

27   Objectives and goals: Writing meaningful goals and SMART objectives, Minnesota Department of Health, updated Mar 3, 2023; https://www.health.state.mn.us/communities/practice/resources/phqitoolbox/objectives.html

28   *What Victor Hugo can teach us about procrastination*, by James Clear, theweek.com, Oct 3, 2016, https://theweek.com/articles/647298/what-victor-hugo-teach-about-procrastination

29   *Victor Hugo, by a Witness of His Life*- by Adèle Hugo and Charles E. Wilbour, (New York: Carleton, 1864).

30   How To Train Like An Olympian, Forbes.com, Jul 8, 2008; https://www.forbes.com/2008/07/08/training-perfect-athlete-olympics08-forbeslife-cx_avd_0708health.html?sh=7aa9ee7579c1

31   *Day in the Life: Michael Phelps*, Jun 7, 2016; https://owaves.com/day-plan/day-life-michael-phelps/

32   Neuroscience Explains Why You Need To Write Down Your Goals If You Actually Want To Achieve Them, by Mark Murphy, Apr 15, 2016, Forbes.com, https://www.forbes.com/sites/markmurphy/2018/04/15/neuroscience-explains-why-you-need-to-write-down-your-goals-if-you-actually-want-to-achieve-them/?sh=796eef6e7905

33   *Implementation Intentions Facilitate Action Control*, by Timothy A. Pychyl, Ph.D., Psychology Today, Jan. 21, 2010.

34   *Making health habitual: the psychology of 'habit-formation' and general practice*, by Benjamin Gardner, Phillippa Lally, Jane Wardle; NIH National Library of Medicine, British Journal of General Practice, Dec 2012

35   Genes, Behavior, and the Social Environment: Moving Beyond the Nature/Nurture Debate, Institute of Medicine (US) Committee on Assessing Interactions Among Social, Behavioral, and Genetic Factors in Health; Hernandez LM, Blazer DG, editors. Washington (DC): National Academies Press (US); 2006.

36   *Reducing the effect of email interruption on employees.* International Journal of Information Management Jackson, T., Dawson, R. and Wilson, D., 2003. , 23(1), pp.55-65

37   *The Daily Word Counts of 19 Famous Writers,* Wordcounter.net; Dec 4, 2017

38   *On Writing: A Memoir of the Craft,* by Stephen King; Scribner, June 2, 2020

39   *Drawing on the Right Side of the Brain* by Betty Edwards, Tarcher; Revised edition (May 1, 1989)

40   Three Ways That Handwriting With A Pen Positively Affects Your Brain; by Nancy Son, Forbes, May 15, 2016.

41   How Handwriting Trains the Brain, by Gwendolyn Bounds; The Wall Street Journal, Oct. 5, 2010.

42   How Handwriting Trains the Brain, by Gwendolyn Bounds; The Wall Street Journal, Oct. 5, 2010.

43   *Effects of Caffeine on Cognitive Performance, Mood, and Alertness in Sleep-Deprived Humans,* by David M. Penetar, Una McCann, David Thorne, Aline Schelling, Cynthia Galinski, Helen Sing, Maria Thomas, and Gregory Belenky; Institute of Medicine (US) Committee on Military Nutrition Research; Marriott BM, editor. Washington (DC): National Academies Press (US); 1994.

44   *How Stimulants Affect the Brain and Behavior*; Treatment Improvement Protocol (TIP) Series, No. 33. Rockville (MD): Substance Abuse and Mental Health Services Administration (US); 1999.

45   Is diet soda bad for you? Know the health risks, by Zawn Villines and reviewed by Katherine Marengo LDN, RD; Medical News Today, July 2019

46   *Be smart, exercise your heart: exercise effects on brain and cognition,* Charles H. Hillman, Kirk I. Erickson and Arthur F. Kramer, Nature Reviews Neuroscience 9, pg. 58-65, Jan. 1, 2008.

47   *How Exercise Affects Your Brain*, by Get-Fit Guy Brock Armstrong, Scientific American, Dec 26, 2018; https://www.scientificamerican.com/article/how-exercise-affects-your-brain/

48   *The antidepressant effect of running is associated with increased hippocampal cell proliferation,* by Bjørnebekk A1, Mathé AA, Brené S., Department of Neuroscience, Karolinska Institutet, Stockholm, Sweden, Int J Neuropsychopharmacology, Sep. 8, 2005, pg. 357-368

49   *Depression and anxiety: Exercise eases symptoms,* By Mayo Clinic Staff; Mayo Clinic; https://www.mayoclinic.org/diseases-conditions/depression/in-depth/depression-and-exercise/art-20046495

50   Exercising to relax: How does exercise reduce stress? Surprising answers to this question and more, Harvard Health Publishing, Harvard Medical School, July 7, 2020

51   *Walking,* by Henry David Thoreau, Watchmaker Publishing, 2010

52   *Walking,* by Henry David Thoreau, Watchmaker Publishing, 2010

53   *A Philosophy of Walking,* by Frederic Gros; Verso; Reprint edition (April 7, 2015)

54   Tchaikovsky, Beethoven, Mahler: They all loved taking long daily walks, By Mason Currey; Slate.com, April 25, 2013; https://slate.com/culture/2013/04/tchaikovsky-beethoven-mahler-they-all-loved-taking-long-daily-walks.html

55   *Walking for good health,* Better Health Channel, https://www.betterhealth.vic.gov.au/health/healthyliving/walking-for-good-health#bhc-content

56   *The Neuroprotective Aspects of Sleep,* by Andy R Eugene, Jolanta Masiak; NIH National Library of Medicine, https://pubmed.ncbi.nlm.nih.gov/26594659/

57   The power of restorative sleep: New research uncovers the connections between sleeping well and staying healthy as we age, By Kirsten Weir; American Psychological Association, October 2017, Vol 48, No. 9.

58   *Challenging Ways Technology Affects Your Sleep,* by The National Sleep Foundation, sleep.org.

59   *Why You Should Find Time to Be Alone With Yourself: Don't confuse loneliness with time by yourself,* by Micaela Marini Higgs; New York Times, Oct 28, 2019 https://www.nytimes.com/2019/10/28/smarter-living/the-benefits-of-being-alone.html

60   *Social Relationships and Health: A Flashpoint for Health Policy,* by Debra Umberson and Jennifer Karas Montez; US National Library of Medicine, National Institutes of Health, Aug 4, 2019

61   *Social isolation, loneliness in older people pose health risks,* National Institute on Aging, April 23, 2019, https://www.nia.nih.gov/news/social-isolation-loneliness-older-people-pose-health-risks

62   *What are the benefits of mindfulness,* By Daphne M. Davis, PhD, and Jeffrey A. Hayes, PhD, American Psychological Association, July/August 2012, Vol 43, No. 7, pg.64; https://www.apa.org/monitor/2012/07-08/ce-corner

63   The No. 1 Habit of Highly Creative People, by Leo Babauta; May 27, 2010, Zenhabits.com

64   *"Isaac Asimov Asks, "How Do People Get New Ideas?,"* by1959 Essay by Isaac Asimov; MIT Technology Review, https://www.technologyreview.com/2014/10/20/169899/isaac-asimov-asks-how-do-people-get-new-ideas/

65   Isaac Asimov Asks, "How Do People Get New Ideas?" A 1959 Essay by Isaac Asimov on Creativity by Isaac Asimov; MIT Technology Review, Oct. 20, 2014

66   Chuck Jones quotes, Goodreads; https://www.goodreads.com/author/quotes/13707.Chuck_Jones

67   Definition of metacognition, Merriam-Webster Dictionary.

68 Groupthink, noun, the Oxford Dictionary.

69 The Power of Imagination, by Remez Sasson; SuccessConsciousness.com

70 Norman Vincent Peale, Brainy Quotes, https://www.brainyquote.com/authors/norman-vincent-peale-quotes

71 Norman Vincent Peale, Brainy Quotes, https://www.brainyquote.com/authors/norman-vincent-peale-quotes

72 Walt Disney quote, Brainy Quotes https://www.brainyquote.com/search_results?q=Walt+Disneyif+you+can+dream+it+you+can+do+it

73 *What Life Means to Einstein: An Interview* by George Sylvester Viereck, The Saturday Evening Post, Oct 26, 1929.

74 *What Imagination Is,* by Jim Davies PH.D, Psychology Today, Jul 11, 2012

75 *Imagination may be more important than knowledge: The eight types of imagination we use*, by Dr. Murray Hunter, University Malaysia Perlis, WiWi-Online.de; Hamburg, Deutschland, 2012; https://works.bepress.com/murray_hunter/18/

76 *The Eight Types of Imagination We Utilize*, Norway Global, The Nordic Page; https://www.tnp.no/norway/global/3163-the-eight-types-of-imagination-we-utilize

77 *Ibid*

78 *Imagination may be more important than knowledge: The eight types of imagination we use*, by Dr. Murray Hunter, University Malaysia Perlis, WiWi-Online.de; Hamburg, Deutschland, 2012; https://works.bepress.com/murray_hunter/18/

79 *Ibid*

80 *The Entrepreneur in Focus: achieve your potential*, Bolton, B., & Thompson, J. (2003). London, Thomson, pp. 92-93.

81 Imagination may be more important than knowledge: The eight types of imagination we use, by Dr. Murray Hunter, University Malaysia Perlis, WiWi-Online.de; Hamburg, Deutschland, 2012; https://works.bepress.com/murray_hunter/18/

82 Ibid

83 *Man and His Symbols*, C. G. Jung, (1964), New York, Dell, P. 27.

84 *The Interpretation of Dreams*, by Sigmund Freud; Nov 4, 1899, 1913 (Macmillan, translation of the German third edition)

85 *Stop Writing Mid-Sentence to Ward Off Writer's Block*, by Kevin Purdy; Lifehacker: Do Everything Better, June 4, 2009; https://lifehacker.com/stop-writing-mid-sentence-to-ward-off-writers-block-5278762

86 *The neurobiological foundation of memory retrieval*, by Paul W. Frankland, Sheena A. Josselyn, and Stefan Köhler; Nature Neuroscience, Sept 24, 2019, https://www.nature.com/articles/s41593-019-0493-1

87 *The Eight Types of Imagination We Utilize*, Norway Global, The Nordic Page; https://www.tnp.no/norway/global/3163-the-eight-types-of-imagination-we-utilize

88 Seeing Is Believing: The Power of Visualization, by A.J. Adams, MAPP, Psychology Today, Dec 3, 2009

89 *How This 10-Minute Routine Will Increase Your Creativity*, by Benjamin Hardy, Ph.D.; Inc. Magazine, https://www.inc.com/benjamin-p-hardy/this-10-minute-routine-before-and-after-sleep-will-increase-your-creativity-and-.html

90 *The Fear of Being Alone*, by Karin Arndt, Ph. D.; Psychology Today, Apr. 8, 2018; https://www.psychologytoday.com/us/blog/hut-her-own/201804/the-fear-being-alone

91 *The Fear of Being Alone*, by Karin Arndt, Ph. D.; Psychology Today, Apr. 8, 2018; https://www.psychologytoday.com/us/blog/hut-her-own/201804/the-fear-being-alone

92 *10 Steps to Serious Goal-Getting from Zig Ziglar*, by Zig Ziglar, Success.com, July 13, 2022; https://www.success.com/ziglar-10-steps-to-serious-goal-getting/

93 Goals: How to Get the Most out of Your Life, by Zig Ziglar, Sound Wisdom, ISBN 978-1640951266